BETTER LIVING THROUGH
ORIGAMI

20 creative paper projects
for a beautiful home

Nellianna van den Baard
and Kenneth Veenenbos

www.sewandso.co.uk

Contents

Introduction

Can you fold a traditional origami crane? Don't worry if the answer is no. Neither could we when we first started. We were inspired to start paper folding when Nellianna's father presented us both with a small origami model, which he had made after taking an origami tutorial that we had given him as a birthday present. We were so blown away by its strength and shadow play that we decided to explore the skill of origami folding for ourselves to design lampshades.

Initially, this was a time of trial and – mostly – error. Folding sheets of baking paper to save on costs, we eventually came up with what are now our best-known pendant lamp designs – the Chestnut and the Moth, which were the first origami-style lampshades on the market when we launched our company, Studio Snowpuppe, back in 2010.

Since we first started our design studio, we have often asked ourselves the question: are we a paper studio making lamps, or a lamp studio making paper lampshades? While writing this book, we have found our answer. Having been given the opportunity to work with paper to create projects other than lamps for the first time, we have discovered that we have a passion to create all sorts of beautiful origami products for the home.

Many of the projects included have been specially designed and cannot be found in the marketplace, although we have also decided to include our popular Moth lampshade and a floor lamp edition of the Thistle, which is our most current design.

Whether you are an experienced origamist or just a beginner, each project is described in a way that is easy to understand and we hope to encourage you to develop your origami skills. Who knows, after you have finished all the projects in this book, you may even be able to fold an origami crane!

Kenneth & Nellianna

STUDIO snowpuppe
BETTER LIVING THROUGH ORIGAMI

How to Use This Book

Before you get started we recommend that you read the following section to ensure that you understand the basics. Here we explain how to follow the instructions and diagrams for the projects in the book. We also list the tools and equipment you'll need to create the projects, with some advice on choosing the correct paper and assembling the designs.

Our method

We learned to design and make our folded interior products by trying different techniques and making a lot of models – this is one of the most enjoyable aspects of working with paper!

It is important to note that the techniques we have used to create the projects featured in this book do not follow the strict rules of traditional origami. These rules state that the project must be folded from a single square of paper without any gluing or cutting.

For our projects we use different shapes and sizes of paper, cut and attach pieces of paper together, and we even add other materials like wood and cord. However, most of the required folds are used in traditional origami.

The terms and descriptions used in this book relate to our personal preferences, so these may be different from what you will find in other books that are solely relating to origami techniques.

Difficulty ratings

Icons are shown at the beginning of each project to indicate the difficulty of the folds and techniques involved. If you're new to folding, we recommend starting with one of the beginner level projects (1 star). Once you've successfully completed the simpler designs, you can progress to the intermediate (2 star), advanced (3 star) and very advanced (4 star) level projects.

Choosing paper

When choosing paper for the projects there are three things to bear in mind – paper weight, colour and size. For each project we advise on the best paper to use, with specific details for paper weight and size given in the requirements list, and advice on colour offered in the introduction.

Paper weight

Paper weight relates to the thickness of the paper, which is measured in grams per square metre (gsm or g/m^2). In this book, we work with three different paper weights:

- **Between 210gsm and 270gsm (medium weight cardstock):** This is used for most of our projects, as it offers the perfect balance of strong but foldable paper.

- **Between 290gsm and 340gsm (heavy cardstock):** This is used for projects that do not have as many folds, as it is more important to use strong paper.

- **Between 150gsm and 190gsm (lightweight, flexible cardstock):** This lighter weight paper is useful for projects where transparency is important, for example where light needs to shine through the paper.

Paper colour

All of the projects in this book look good in white, but you may prefer to use coloured paper to coordinate with your existing home décor. Advice on choosing the most appropriate colour is provided in the introduction for the relevant project.

If you choose a coloured paper, make sure that it is fully coloured (i.e., the paper is coloured on both sides and also has a coloured core) as some coloured papers can be layered with white. You will get the best results using a paper that is made from coloured paper pulp.

Paper size

You will need to cut paper to specific sizes for each project based on the measurements given in the requirements list. It is important that this is done accurately to ensure the best results. We recommend using a sharp craft blade with a metal ruler.

For the projects featured in this book the maximum size of paper we use is 1000 x 700mm. This is very close to the International Organization for Standardization (ISO) B1 size, which is widely available from stationers. Of course you can always use a smaller size, but in some cases this may mean that you will need to attach more pieces of paper together.

Tools and equipment

The following list covers the main tools and materials that we work with for the projects featured in this book. Any specific materials or additional tools that may be required are listed with the individual project instructions:

- Cutting mat
- Bone folder
- Scoring tool
- Metal ruler
- Geo triangle
- Craft blade
- Scissors
- Cord
- Double-sided tape: 6mm, 10mm
- Masking tape
- Wood glue
- Hole punch: 2mm, 4mm
- Lighter

Making the projects

Each of the projects features its own requirements list with specific details of the paper, materials and additional tools you will need. The instructions for every project are divided into three main sections – scoring, folding and assembly.

Scoring

The first stage of creating your chosen design is to score the pattern. For each project there will either be a template to trace and/or instructions for various lines to score onto your pre-cut pieces of paper. Take your time when scoring the lines to ensure that you do not tear or damage the paper.

Mark and score the vertical and horizontal lines first (see tip), and then mark and score the diagonal lines between the intersections, scoring each piece of paper on one side.

Instead of drawing the lines with a pencil first, we prefer to directly draw onto the paper with a scoring tool or the back of a knife, making a dent in the paper at the location of the points to be marked. If you do use a pencil, draw softly so the line is easy to erase.

Once all of the lines shown on the diagram have been scored, prepare any edges that need to be taped or glued and punch holes if necessary. Make sure that you have extended the scored lines onto the assembly tab. This is important because the assembly tab will also need to be folded in order to be able to attach the ends of the paper together nicely.

Folding

Before you start to fold your chosen paper, make a model of one segment (see Understanding diagram, Segment Diagram) with a piece of scrap paper to practise the folds. The best way to learn is through practice, as you will begin to understand the diagrams better and the text will help to guide you.

There are three stages involved in folding the projects:

- Pre-folding
- Pleating
- Changing direction

These are explained further in the Techniques section (see Techniques), along with an explanation of the basic folds: mountain and valley.

Assembly

Once all of the lines have been folded, there is often assembly involved to attach the folded pieces of paper together. This stage needs a lot of care and attention to ensure that your finished project looks professional.

We use double-sided tape, glue and cord to attach the pieces of paper together. The most appropriate method is indicated in the instructions for each project, but here is some general advice to bear in mind:

- **Double-sided tape:** Quality is far more important than quantity, so it is worth spending time searching for the strongest double-sided tape you can find. For the projects featured in this book we mostly use 10mm-wide double-sided tape.
- **Glue:** The only glue that we use is basic wood glue. Wood glue doesn't dry particularly quickly, but it creates a permanent seal and dries completely clear. This makes it extremely reliable and ensures a neat finish, even if there are spillages.
- **Cord:** Using cord allows flexibility, as you can pull the folded paper model together and then open it again. This enables you to change the light bulb in a lampshade and to put new batteries in the standing clock. We use braided flying line, as you are able to melt the ends of the cord in order to prevent it from fraying. A length of 1 metre should be sufficient for the knots (see Techniques: Sliding Knot).

Understanding the diagrams

Depending on the project, we use a combination of diagrams to explain the patterns. For every step we note the relevant diagram to offer a visual reference for each instruction.

Different colours are used on the diagrams to identify the techniques required. The key seen here (see Key) explains what the different colours stand for.

Overview Diagram

This diagram shows an overview of the full paper size that is needed. It features all of the folding lines, intersections, tabs that need to be taped or glued and any holes that need to be punched. It also shows which folding lines make up one segment and how many segments each sheet of paper will have.

If more than one piece of paper in the same size is required, this diagram represents only one of the pieces.

This Overview Diagram example shows a piece of paper measuring 330 x 105mm. It contains eight folded segments, with punched holes along the bottom edges and a 10mm-wide assembly tab covered with double-sided tape along one side.

Key

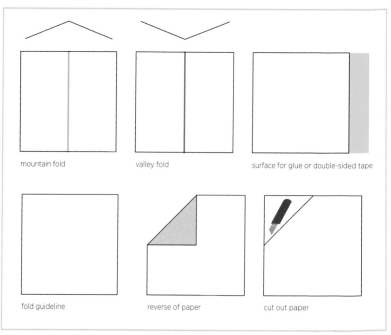

mountain fold   valley fold   surface for glue or double-sided tape

fold guideline   reverse of paper   cut out paper

Overview Diagram

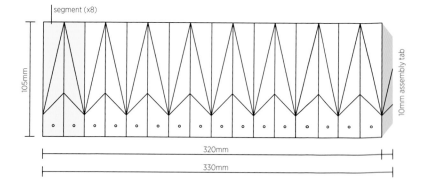

segment (x8)

105mm

10mm assembly tab

320mm

330mm

Segment Diagram

This diagram shows how the folding lines should be measured for each segment. All of the lines are coloured to indicate their purpose (see Key).

The segment diagram shows what each folding line should be (valley or mountain fold) for the final model.

We recommend that, before you start to fold your chosen paper, you make a model of one segment with a piece of scrap paper to practise the folds.

This Segment Diagram example shows a segment measuring 40 x 105mm. It contains vertical folding lines, with diagonal folding lines across the intersections and punched holes along the bottom edge.

Pleating Diagram

This diagram shows how the vertical scored lines of each segment need to be folded when pleating the paper. This can be a valley fold (blue) or a mountain fold (orange).The pleated paper is the start point for changing the direction of the folds in the folding steps for each project (see Techniques: Folding, Changing Direction). It should be noted, however, that as you will start pleating at one edge of the paper, this edge of the pleated paper isn't folded and only becomes a valley or mountain fold when the pleated paper is joined with the assembly tab(s). Effectively you cannot fold the first edge of the paper.

Template

Projects that require unusually shaped pieces of paper have their own template (see Templates). If a template has been provided for a particular project, this will be indicated in the scoring instructions. Templates are shown at actual size and can therefore be copied and traced directly onto your paper.

Full size templates for all the projects in this book are available from a dedicated online space (see Suppliers).

Segment Diagram

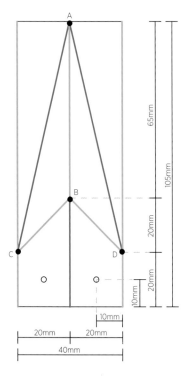

Pleating Diagram

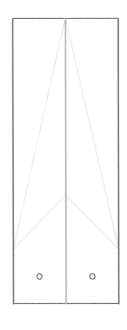

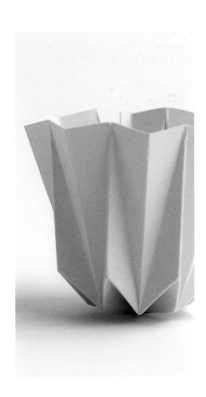

FOR THE TABLE

Triangles Vase

A bouquet of fresh flowers may last only up to a few weeks, but this attractive origami vase filled with dried blooms will brighten your home for years! We love the gold tones and the structure of the dried leaves. You can make the vase in one colour or make the two parts in different shades for a quirky look. We chose a paper that is coloured on the front and white on the reverse to give more dimension.

YOU WILL NEED

- 24 pieces of 210-270gsm paper, 120 x 65mm
- Straight-sided glass vase with an inner diameter of 80mm

Scoring

Make a copy of the Triangles Vase template (see Templates) and fix it temporarily onto one of the 24 pieces of paper with masking tape. Trace the outline of the template and carefully cut out with a craft blade and a metal ruler.

Score vertical lines at 20mm, 60mm and 100mm from the left-hand edge of the piece (see Segment Diagram).

Score a diagonal line to join the tops of the second and third vertical lines to create a tab (see Segment Diagram). Apply 6mm double-sided tape above this line on the front of the paper (labelled B on the Segment Diagram).

Repeat with the remaining pieces of paper to create a total of 24 folded segments.

Segment Diagram

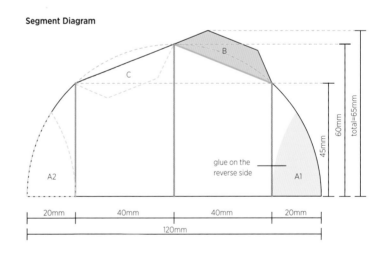

Folding

Valley fold the scored blue lines and mountain fold the scored orange line as shown on Segment Diagram.

Fold the two outer edges in towards each other, apply glue to the area where they overlap (labelled A1 and A2 on Segment Diagram) and secure.

Repeat for the remaining segments to create 24 identical triangular pieces (see Diagram 1), 12 to make the top part of the vase and 12 to make the bottom part.

You can overlap A1 and A2 from left to right or right to left just as long as you are consistent.

Assembly

Remove the backing from the double-sided tape on one of the triangular pieces and attach the tab to the reverse of another triangular piece (labelled B and C on Segment Diagram).

Continue until you have created a closed circle made up of 12 triangular pieces (see Diagram 2). Then repeat the process to create another closed circle with the remaining 12 folded pieces.

These two circles are the two separate parts for the top and bottom of the vase, and one becomes the top of the vase when it is turned upside down.

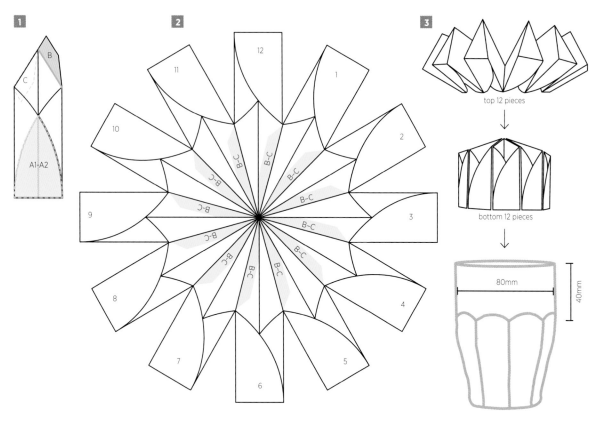

1

B

C

A1-A2

2

12
11
10
9
8
7
6
5
4
3
2
1

B~C
B~C
B~C
B~C
B~C
B~C
B~C
B~C
B~C
B~C
B~C

3

top 12 pieces

bottom 12 pieces

80mm

40mm

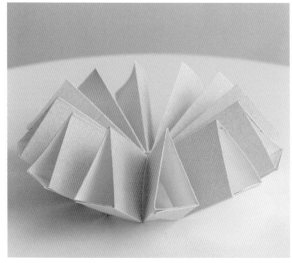

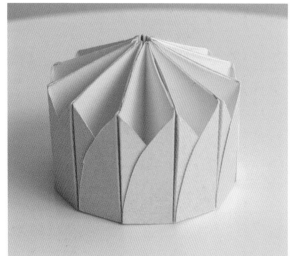

Kaleidoscope Coaster

A small, square picture frame is the perfect container for this origami decoration, which doubles up as an eye-catching coaster. Place an attractive glass on its transparent surface to see the folds reflected and deflected, just like a real kaleidoscope. The frame's transparent layer will protect the origami from spillages. We chose blue paper for our coaster, but you could make a set in various colours.

YOU WILL NEED

- 1 piece of 150-190gsm paper, 160 x 152mm
- Picture frame with inner dimensions of 100 x 100mm

Scaling the pattern

Our instructions are for an origami model to fit inside a picture frame with inner dimensions of 100 x 100mm, but you can scale up the template to fit a larger frame using the following formulae.

Scaling factor = width of your picture frame ÷ 100mm

For example, for a picture frame with inner dimensions of 200 x 200mm, the scaling factor is 200mm ÷ 100mm, which is 2, so the template needs to be scaled to twice its size.

Distance between the parallel lines = scaling factor x 7mm

For example, for a picture frame with inner dimensions of 200 x 200mm, the distance between the parallel lines will be 2 x 7mm = 14mm.

Scoring

Make a copy of the template (see Templates) and fix it temporarily onto your paper with masking tape. Trace the outline of the template and carefully cut out with a craft blade and a metal ruler.

Score lines from point O to point B, C, D and E.

Score lines from point A to B, B to C, C to D and D to E.

Score the horizontal lines for surface OCD, measuring 7mm between the parallel lines (see Overview Diagram). (Note: the distance between the parallel lines will depend on the size of your picture frame; see Scaling the Pattern.)

Rotate the paper clockwise by 72 degrees, so point D becomes point C, and score the horizontal lines for surface ODE as before. Continue to score the remaining horizontal lines, rotating the paper clockwise by 72 degrees each time.

At this stage your model has a pentagon shape, but once folded and assembled it will end up as a square shape. Apply 6mm double-sided tape to the assembly tab (see Overview Diagram).

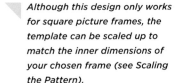

Although this design only works for square picture frames, the template can be scaled up to match the inner dimensions of your chosen frame (see Scaling the Pattern).

Folding

Pre-fold the scored lines OB, OC, OD and OE in both directions, starting with a valley fold and finishing with a mountain fold.

Pre-fold the scored lines AB, BC, CD and DE in both directions as labelled s1 on Diagram 1 to run all the way around your model, including the assembly tab. Continue to pre-fold each of the parallel scored lines (s2, s3, s4, s5, s6 and s7) in turn, in both directions (see Diagrams 2-4).

Valley fold the scored line s1; note that the lines that run from point O to line s1 will become mountain folds (see Diagram 1).

Mountain fold the scored line s2; note that the lines that run from point O to line s2 will become valley folds (see Diagram 2).

Valley fold the scored line s3; note that the lines that run from point O to line s3 will become mountain folds (see Diagram 3).

Continue to fold the remaining scored parallel lines to this pattern as follows: s4 mountain fold; s5 valley fold; s6 mountain fold; s7 valley fold (see Diagram 4).

Overview Diagram

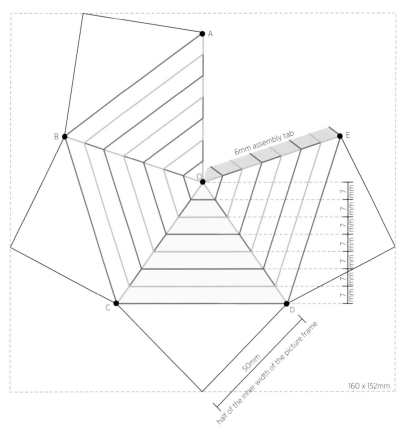

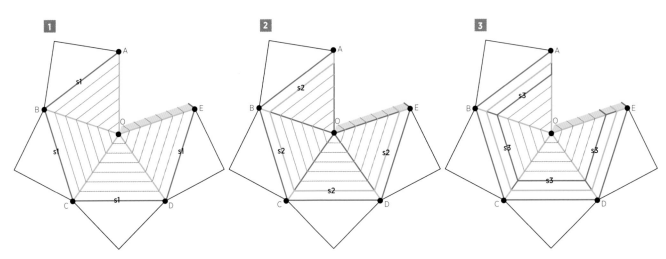

Assembly

Remove the backing from the double-sided tape and attach the ends of the model together to create a square shape, ensuring that the taped edge is on the reverse of the model, so that points A and E join to become point A/E (see Diagram 5).

Mountain fold lines BC, CD, DA/E and A/EB over an angle of 90 degrees (i.e., over the edge of the table), so that you can make the folds of your paper model sharper by squeezing at the points marked in Diagram 6. Then release to revert to the square shape seen in Diagram 5, and place the paper model in your picture frame, where it is displayed as a diamond shape.

When folding the scored lines, it is easier if you start at the edge that is opposite the assembly tab.

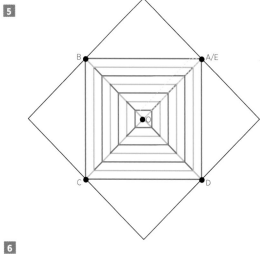

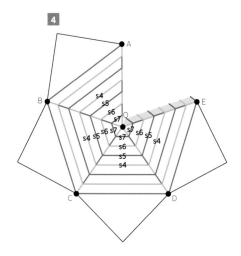

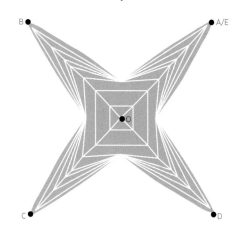

Pencil Pot

This little pot is the perfect desktop accessory, giving you a place to keep all your favourite pens and pencils close to hand. It's a great example of modular origami, where two identically folded units are attached together with glue to form one structure. We've made both parts from pale pink paper, but you could make the top in one colour and the bottom in another, if you choose to.

YOU WILL NEED

- 2 pieces of 210-270gsm paper, 208 x 180mm

Scoring

Make a copy of the template (see Templates) and fix it temporarily onto each piece of paper with masking tape. Trace the outline of the template onto the paper and carefully cut out with a craft blade and a metal ruler.

Take one piece of paper for the top part of the pot and referring to the measurements on the Overview Diagram: Top, score the horizontal lines, using the cut out corners of your cut out shape to help guide you.

Rotate the paper clockwise by 60 degrees, so triangle A is now at the bottom left-hand corner and score the horizontal lines as before.

Rotate the paper clockwise by 60 degrees one last time and score the remaining horizontal lines.

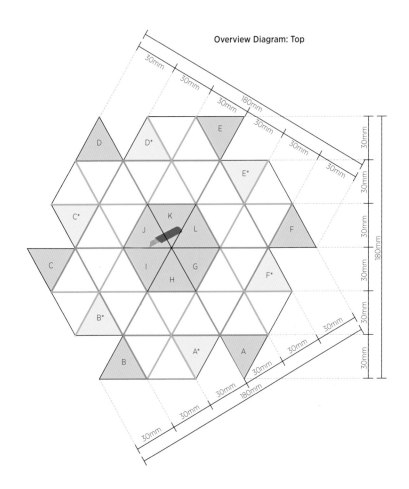

Overview Diagram: Top

Take your remaining piece of paper and repeat to score the fold lines for the bottom part of the pot, but do not score lines across the centre hexagon shape (see Overview Diagram: Bottom), which is the pot base.

Returning to the scored paper for the top part of the pot, use a craft blade and a metal ruler to cut the black lines in the centre hexagon shape (see Overview Diagram:Top); this creates the assembly tabs to attach the top part to the bottom part after folding.

Folding

For the bottom part of the model:

▷ Fold all the scored lines in the direction as indicated in the Overview Diagram.

▷ Glue triangle surface A to the reverse side of surface A*, and repeat to glue B to B*, C to C*, D to D*, E to E*, and F to F* (see Diagram 1).

Overview Diagram: Bottom

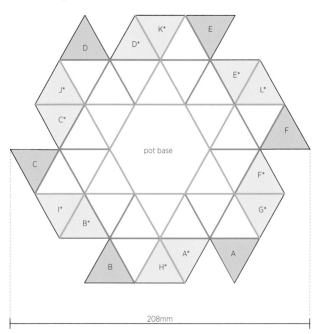

208mm

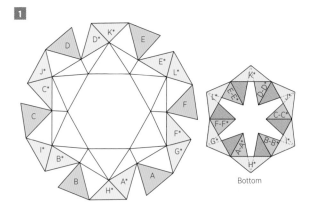

Bottom

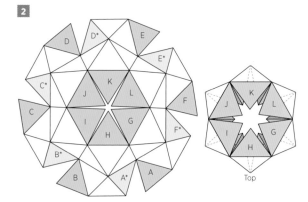

Top

For the top part of the model:

▷ Referring to Diagram 2, first repeat steps as for the bottom part of the model.

▷ Then fold the triangle surfaces marked G, H, I, J, K and L as indicated in the Overview Diagram: Top, so they point downwards to give you the assembly tabs to attach the top part of the model to the bottom part.

Assembly

To attach the top part of the model to the bottom part, put a little glue on the outside of triangles G, H, I, J, K and L on the top part of the model and attach these to the reverse of triangle surfaces G*, H*, I*, J*, K* and L* on the bottom part of the model (see Diagram 3). Your pencil pot is now ready to be filled with pencils.

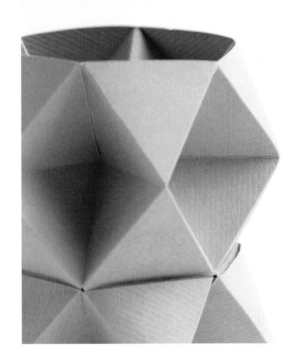

3

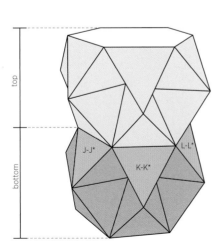

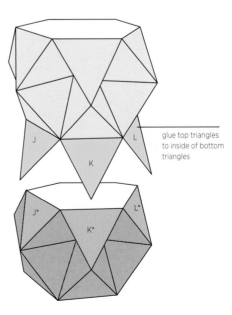

glue top triangles to inside of bottom triangles

Mini Plant Pot

One day, when we have more time, we'd like to try our hand at pottery, but till then we'll have to satisfy ourselves with this faux ceramic plant pot duo. The cup is a great way to disguise a plastic pot and it sits neatly inside a specially designed saucer. We chose a soft blue paper to emphasize the distinctive folds, but any pastel colour would work just as well. You could make these items separately.

YOU WILL NEED

- 1 piece of 210–270gsm paper, 330 x 105mm for the cup
- 1 piece of 210–270gsm paper, 530 x 105mm for the saucer
- Small plant pot without draining holes, max. 60mm high, 70mm diameter at top, 45mm diameter at base

Cup
Scoring

Score vertical lines at intervals of 20mm along the length of the paper (see Overview Diagram). There will be a 10mm section remaining on the right-hand edge, which will become an assembly tab. Each set of two 20mm scored sections forms a segment (see Segment Diagram).

Starting with the first segment, referring to the measurements given in the Segment Diagram, mark points A, B, C and D, then score diagonal lines between the marked points as shown (see Segment Diagram). Repeat this process for each segment and continue to partially mark and score lines across the assembly tab section (see Overview Diagram).

Apply double-sided tape to the 10mm section on the right-hand edge of the scored piece (see Overview Diagram). Cut the corners of the assembly tab at a 45 degree angle.

Use a 2mm hole punch to punch holes 10mm in from the side and bottom edges in each 20mm scored section (see Overview Diagram and Segment Diagram).

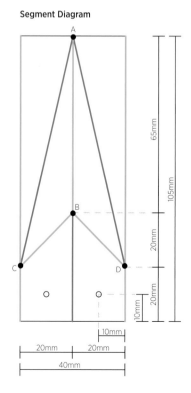

Segment Diagram

Folding

Pre-fold each of the scored vertical lines in both directions.

Fold the paper vertically along the central scored line of the first segment. Pre-fold all the diagonal scored lines of the segment in both directions. Repeat this process for the remaining segments.

Next pleat the paper along the scored vertical lines of each segment as indicated on the Pleating Diagram (see Techniques: Folding, Pleating).

Starting with the first segment and referring to Techniques: Folding, Changing Direction, valley fold the top two scored diagonal lines (labelled d1 on Diagram 1). Repeat for remaining segments.

Starting with the first segment, mountain fold the bottom two scored diagonal lines (labelled d2 on Diagram 2). Repeat for remaining segments.

Overview Diagram

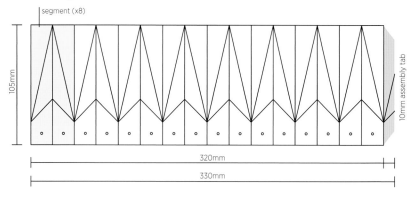

segment (x8)

105mm

10mm assembly tab

320mm

330mm

Pleating Diagram

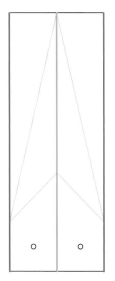

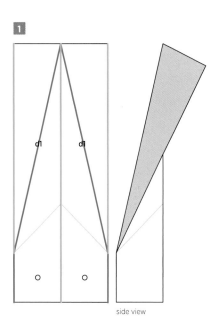

1

d1   d1

side view

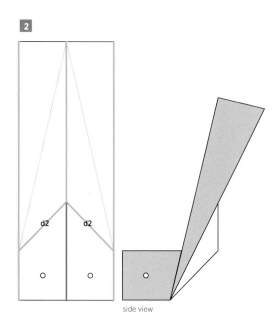

2

d2   d2

side view

Assembly

Remove the backing from the double-sided tape at the end of the folded piece and attach the ends of the model together to create the cup shape, ensuring that the taped edge is on the reverse of the cup.

Thread a 1 metre length of cord through the holes along the bottom edge of the cup. Gently pull the cord to close the gap at the base of the cup and secure by tying a sliding knot (see Techniques: Sliding Knot). To keep the cup shape secured, make a third knot close to knot 2, then trim off the remaining cord length. Place your plant pot inside the cup (see Diagram 3).

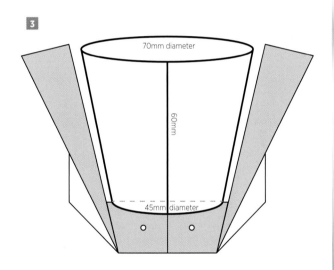

3

70mm diameter

60mm

45mm diameter

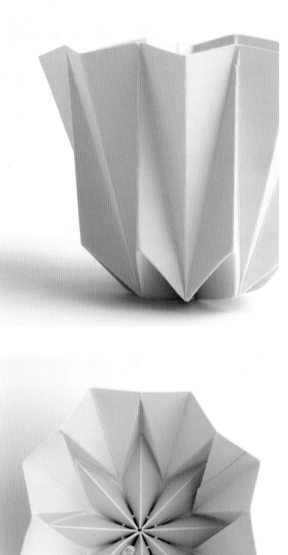

Segment Diagram

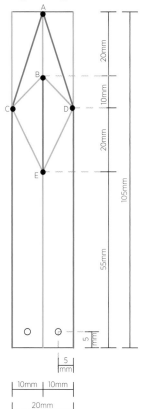

Saucer

Scoring

Score vertical lines at intervals of 10mm along the length of the paper (see Overview Diagram). There will be a 10mm section remaining on the right-hand edge, which will become an assembly tab. Each set of two 10mm scored sections forms a segment (see Segment Diagram).

Starting with the first segment, referring to the measurements given in the Segment Diagram, mark points A, B, C, D and E, then score diagonal lines between the marked points as shown (see Segment Diagram). Repeat this process for each segment and continue to partially mark and score lines across the assembly tab section (see Overview Diagram).

Apply double-sided tape to the 10mm section on the right-hand edge of the scored piece (see Overview Diagram). Cut the corners of the assembly tab at a 45 degree angle.

Use a 2mm hole punch to punch holes 5mm in from the side and bottom edges in each 10mm scored section (see Overview Diagram and Segment Diagram).

Folding

Pre-fold each of the scored vertical lines in both directions.

Fold the paper vertically along the central scored line of the first segment. Then pre-fold all the diagonal scored lines of the segment in both directions. Repeat for remaining segments.

Pleat paper along scored vertical lines of each segment as indicated on the Pleating Diagram (see Techniques: Folding, Pleating).

Starting with the first segment and referring to Techniques: Folding, Changing Direction, valley fold the top two scored diagonal lines (labelled d1 on Diagram 1). Repeat for remaining segments.

Starting with the first segment, mountain fold the middle two scored diagonal lines (labelled d2 on Diagram 2). Repeat for remaining segments.

Starting with the first segment, mountain fold the bottom two scored diagonal lines (labelled d3 on Diagram 3). Repeat for remaining segments.

Overview Diagram

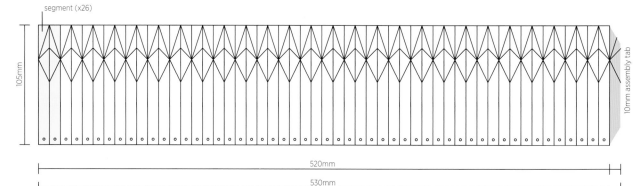

Assembly

Remove the backing from the double-sided tape at the end of the folded piece and attach the ends of the model together to create the saucer shape, ensuring that the taped edge is on the reverse of the saucer.

Thread a 1 metre length of cord through the holes and gently pull the cord to close the gap at the base of the saucer and secure by tying a sliding knot (see Techniques: Sliding Knot). To keep the saucer shape secured, make a third knot close to knot 2, then trim off the remaining cord length. Place cup inside the saucer: the weight of the cup will keep the saucer in the right shape.

Pleating Diagram

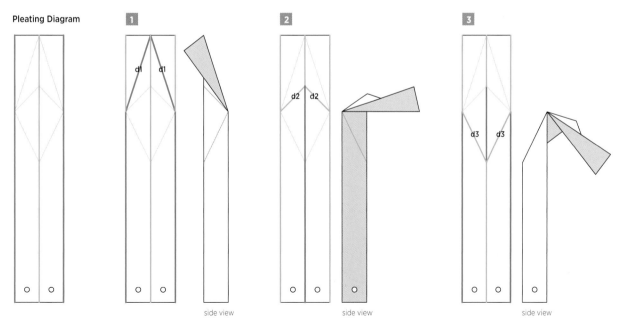

side view

side view

side view

Standing Clock

This small clock has been specially designed for a bedside table. The front has a folded star design, where each ray represents one of the numbers on a clock face, and the model stands securely on the folded back structure. While some of the folds are sharply defined, others are only slightly visible, and it is this, together with our choice of a lilac paper, that gives the clock its subtle folded effect.

YOU WILL NEED

- 1 piece of 210-270gsm paper, 490 x 208mm
- An analogue clock mechanism with a spindle length of 31mm (see Suppliers)
- A minute hand around 47mm and an hour hand around 36mm (see Suppliers)

Scoring

Score vertical lines at intervals of 20mm along the length of the paper (see Overview Diagram). There will be a 10mm section remaining on the right-hand edge, which will become an assembly tab. Each set of two 20mm scored sections forms a segment (see Segment Diagram).

Score the horizontal line that runs across the width of the paper (see Overview Diagram), referring to the measurements given on the Segment Diagram.

Starting with the first segment, referring to the measurements given in the Segment Diagram, mark points A, B, C, D, E, F, G, H, I, J, K and L, then score diagonal lines between the marked points as shown (see Segment Diagram). Repeat for each segment and continue to partially mark and score lines across the assembly tab section (see Overview Diagram).

Apply double-sided tape to the 10mm section on the right-hand edge of the scored piece (see Overview Diagram). Cut the corners of the assembly tab at a 45 degree angle.

Use a 2mm hole punch to punch holes that are 10mm in from the side and bottom edges in each 20mm scored section (see Overview Diagram and Segment Diagram). Repeat this process to punch the holes along the top edge of the paper.

> *Once positioned, the clock will stay securely in place and will not rotate, but when dusting or replacing the battery be sure to reposition the clock so that it tells the right time.*

Segment Diagram

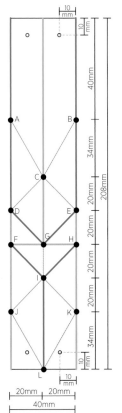

Overview Diagram

segment (x12)

208mm

10mm assembly tab

480mm

490mm

Folding

Pre-fold each of the scored vertical lines in both directions, then pre-fold the scored horizontal line in both directions.

Fold the paper vertically along the central scored line of the first segment. Pre-fold all the diagonal scored lines of the segment in both directions. Repeat this process for the remaining segments.

Pleat paper along scored vertical lines of each segment as indicated on the Pleating Diagram (see Techniques: Folding, Pleating).

Mountain fold the scored horizontal line (labelled h1 on Diagram 1) across the full width of the paper and fold over an angle of 90 degrees (i.e., over the edge of the table).

Starting with the first segment and referring to Techniques: Folding, Changing Direction, valley fold the two scored diagonal lines labelled d1 on Diagram 1. Repeat for remaining segments.

Pleating Diagram 1

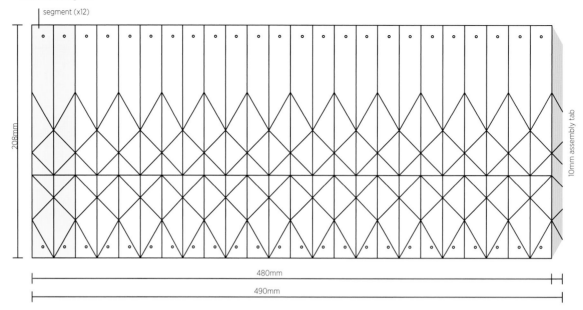

h1

d1 d1

side view

3D perspective

Starting with the first segment, valley fold the two scored diagonal lines labelled d2 on Diagram 2. Repeat for remaining segments.

Assembly

Remove the backing from the double-sided tape at the end of the folded piece and attach the ends of the model together to create the shape of a tube, ensuring that the taped edge is on the reverse.

Thread a 1 metre length of cord through the holes at the bottom of the folded piece (see Overview Diagram) and gently pull the cord to shape the clock face until just a small hole remains (see Diagram 3); secure the ends of the cord by tying a sliding knot (see Techniques: Sliding Knot).

Assemble the clock mechanism by placing the spindle through the hole in the centre of the folded clock face. Use the screw provided to secure the mechanism in place (see Diagram 4).

To ensure that the clock face keeps its shape so that the clock hands can rotate freely, fill the finished model with scrunched up balls of paper or cloth.

Thread a 1 metre length of cord through the holes at the top of the folded piece (see Overview Diagram) and gently pull the cord to close the back of the standing clock; secure the ends of the cord by tying a sliding knot (see Techniques: Sliding Knot).

Attach the minute and hour hands to the clock face to finish.

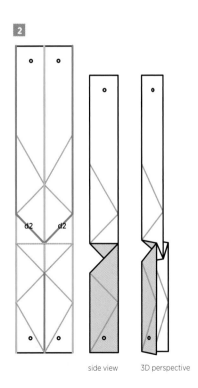

2

d2   d2

side view   3D perspective

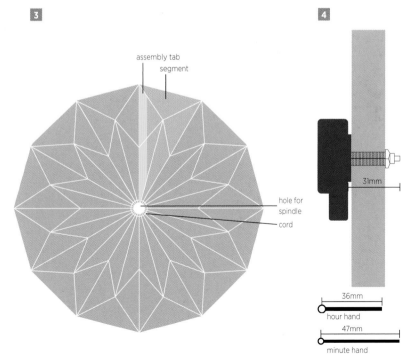

3

assembly tab
segment

hole for spindle
cord

4

31mm

36mm
hour hand

47mm
minute hand

Thistle Lamp

This is our first lampshade design for a floor lamp although it could just as easily be used as a lampshade for a large table lamp. Inspired by the form and texture of the thistle plant, the lampshade is curved with papercut 'spikes'. The paper slits allow the straight folds to be manipulated into the distinctive shape, creating a surprising lighting effect. White paper must be used to let the light shine through and it is important that it does not tear easily, so test before starting.

YOU WILL NEED

- 2 pieces of 210-270gsm paper, 980 x 700mm (important: use a paper that does not tear easily)
- Floor lamp base (see Suppliers)
- Metal ring, 150mm diameter with a rod thickness of 4mm (see Suppliers)
- Shade carrier and duplex ringset (see Suppliers) and LED light bulb (see Techniques: Lamp Safety)

Scoring

Starting at the left-hand edge of one of the pieces of paper, score the vertical lines that run from the top to the bottom of the paper (see Overview Diagram), referring to the measurements given at the base of the Segment Diagram. There will be a 20mm section remaining on the right-hand edge, which will become an assembly tab.

Each segment has two 30mm scored sections at its centre, and the 20mm sections on either side of these centre sections are shared equally between neighbouring segments, so that each segment has 10mm sections at either side of the centre sections (see Overview Diagram and Segment Diagram).

Repeat with the other piece of paper to give you a total of 24 scored segments.

Overview Diagram

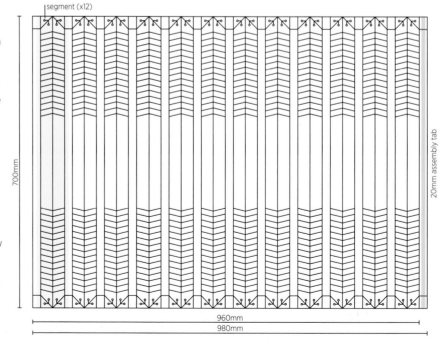

segment (x12)

700mm

20mm assembly tab

960mm

980mm

For each segment:

▷ Mark points A, B, C, D, E and F, referring to the measurements given on the Segment Diagram, then score diagonal lines between the marked points as shown (see Segment Diagram).

▷ Score the horizontal lines between the marked points (see Segment Diagram). and continue to partially mark and score the horizontal lines across the assembly tab section (see Overview Diagram).

▷ Referring to the measurements given on the Segment Diagram detail, mark the angled (black) cutting lines in the centre sections of the segment, making sure that the lines are angled downwards in the top half of the segment and upwards in the bottom half of the segment (as seen on the Segment Diagram Detail). Cut along the marked cutting lines with a craft blade and a metal ruler, taking care not to extend the cut lines beyond the 30mm sections.

Apply 10mm double-sided tape to the centre of the 20mm section on the right-hand edge of each piece of paper (see Overview Diagram).

Use a 4mm hole punch to punch the holes to the far left of each segment along the top edge of the paper (this is the hole labelled 1 in Diagram 2). It is important to be very precise with the hole location, so refer to the measurements given on the Segment Diagram detail, but remember that at this stage you are only punching the first of the four holes.

Repeat to punch the holes to the far left of each segment along the bottom edge of the paper (this is the hole labelled 1 in Diagram 2).

Segment Diagram   **Segment Diagram Detail**

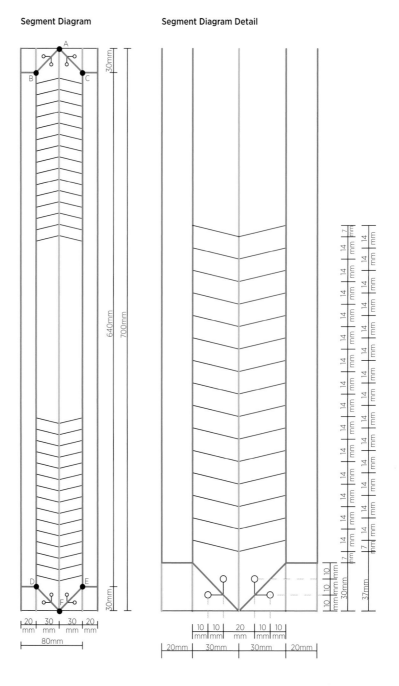

Folding

For each piece of paper, pre-fold each of the scored vertical lines in both directions, then pleat paper along scored vertical lines of each segment as indicated on the Pleating Diagram (see Techniques: Folding, Pleating). The result will be pleated paper pieces with 20mm-wide flat sections alternating with mountain sections. As it is not possible to compress the paper, you must try to fold all vertical folds as tightly as possible to sharpen these folds.

For each segment:

▷ Fold the paper vertically along the central scored line and use a 4mm hole punch to punch the top right hole along the top edge of the segment (the hole labelled 4 in Diagram 3a) and the bottom right hole along the bottom edge of the segment.

> *As holes 1 and 4 overlap, you can punch hole 4 by placing your hole punch through hole 1.*

▷ Valley fold the two scored lines labelled d1 on Diagram 1.

▷ Valley fold the two scored lines labelled d2 on Diagram 1.

Now punch the remaining holes along the top edge of the paper. To do this, fold the diagonal valley folds so that the holes on the outer edge of the segment (holes 1 and 4) overlap with the hole positions on the inner edge of the segment (holes 2 and 3). As all four holes overlap, you can punch holes 2 and 3 simultaneously by placing your hole punch through either hole 1 or hole 4. Refer to Diagram 3b for making holes.

Pleating Diagram

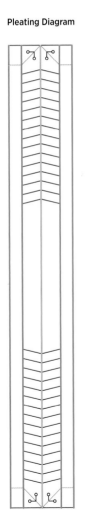

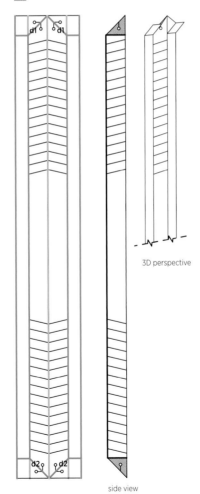

3D perspective

side view

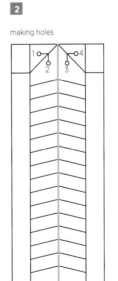

2

making holes

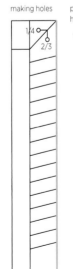

3a

making holes

3b

position for punching holes 2/3

3D perspective

Repeat to punch the remaining holes along the bottom edge of the paper.

Unfold the diagonal folds from making holes so that this part of the paper now lies flat.

For each segment, refer to Diagram 2 and take care **not** to cut through scored diagonal lines labelled d1 and d2 on Diagram 1 as you:

▷ Mark and cut the horizontal black lines that run from hole 1 to scored diagonal lines d1 and d2.

▷ Mark and cut the vertical black lines that run from hole 2 to scored diagonal lines d1 and d2.

▷ Mark and cut the horizontal black lines that run from hole 4 to scored diagonal lines d1 and d2.

▷ Mark and cut the vertical black lines that run from hole 3 to scored diagonal lines d1 and d2.

Assembly

Remove the backing from the double-sided tape on the right-hand edge of one folded piece and attach to the left-hand edge of the other piece to create one long strip of folded paper.

Remove the backing from the double-sided tape on the right-hand edge of the second folded piece and attach the ends of the model together to create a tube shape.

Place the model on a clean work surface, making sure that there is enough space for you to walk all the way around it.

Refold the scored diagonal lines d1 (see Diagram 1). Turn the model upside down and try to get the bottom of the model to fall into a curved shape (see Diagram 4), then refold the scored diagonal lines d2.

Take the metal ring and clip it into the four holes along the folded edge of each segment (see Diagram 5). As you do so, you will notice that your tube shape will start to change into a sphere. As you work your way around the model, it becomes a little more difficult to attach the folded segments to the metal ring, so gently and carefully squeeze the already attached segments together to give you space to add the rest of the folded segments.

As you reach halfway, make sure to fold both the folded segment you are currently attaching as well as the following segment too, and make sure that the shape of both segments are curved like the segments you have already attached.

As you reach the end, make sure all the remaining segments are correctly folded and positioned to enable you to attach the very last folds to the metal ring (see Diagram 6).

Gently turn the model right way up to clip the metal ring at the top of the duplex ringset into the holes along the top edge of the lampshade.

It is important to read the safety instructions before installing the lampshade as seen in Diagram 7 (see Techniques: Lamp Safety). Make sure that the floor lamp is unplugged from the socket. Remove the ring beneath the light bulb fitting. Place the bottom metal ring of the shade carrier over the light bulb fitting and reattach the ring. Place the bottom metal ring of the duplex ringset at the top metal ring of the shade carrier. The lampshade will fall into its shape but this can take up to a day. If you don't want to wait, you can fold the central folded lines of each segment once more while the lampshade is hanging. Then fit a light bulb, put the plug back in the socket and switch on the power.

4

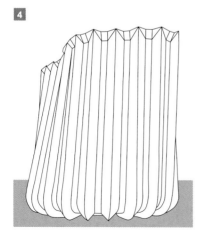

5

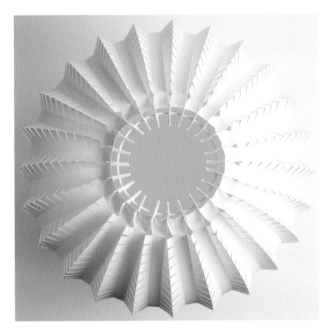

6

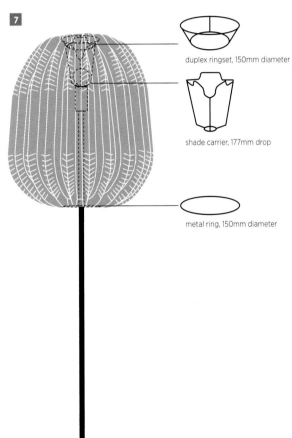

metal ring, 150mm diameter

7

duplex ringset, 150mm diameter

shade carrier, 177mm drop

metal ring, 150mm diameter

Picture Frame

A paper-folded picture frame is the ideal way to make a lightweight frame that is just the right size to fit your favourite illustration. Better still, as there is no heavy glass involved, there's no need to drill a large hole in your wall as a small hook will be fine to hang it from. So now you can change the pictures on your wall as often as you choose.

YOU WILL NEED

- 1 piece of 210-270gsm paper, 806 x 40mm
- An A5 illustration

 Before you start, refer to Calculating the Paper Size.

Calculating the paper size

Our instructions are for making a picture frame to fit around an A5 format portrait illustration with a height of 210mm and a width of 148mm (see the zebra illustration in the photograph), but it is easy to adapt the measurements to custom fit the size of your illustration. Each picture frame starts with a long strip of paper, and the size of the paper strip is determined by the following dimensions: the height and width of your illustration and the preferred depth of your picture frame border (see Overview Diagram). To calculate the size of your paper strip, use the following formulae:

Width of paper = depth of picture frame border x 2:
First determine the preferred depth of your frame border. In our example, the width of the paper is 40mm for a picture frame border of 20mm deep.

Perimeter = 2 x (h+w): To establish the length of your paper strip, you must first determine the perimeter measurement of your illustration, which is the length of the outer edge of your picture. Add the picture height and the picture width, then multiply by 2. In our example, the perimeter of our illustration is 2 x (210mm + 148mm) = 716mm.

Length of paper = perimeter + 4 x depth of picture frame border: To be able to fold the picture frame corners, you need to allow a measurement that is the same as the depth of the frame border for each corner. In our example, which has a picture frame depth of 20mm, this is 80mm. This measurement is then added to the perimeter calculation, so for our picture frame the calculation is 716mm + (4 x 20mm) = 796mm. Finally, add 10mm to the length of the paper strip for the assembly tab (see the 10mm area covered with double-sided tape at the top of the Overview Diagram). So, in our example, the total length of the strip of paper will be 796 + 10 = 806mm.

So, the final dimensions of our paper strip is 806mm long by 40mm wide (see Overview Diagram).

Note: as most papers have a maximum length of 1000mm, we have been able to make our A5 picture frame from just one sheet of paper, but if your length calculation exceeds 1000mm, you will need to attach two paper strips to give you your length, and if this is the case, you will need to add an additional 10mm to the paper strip length to allow for joining the paper strips together.

Overview Diagram

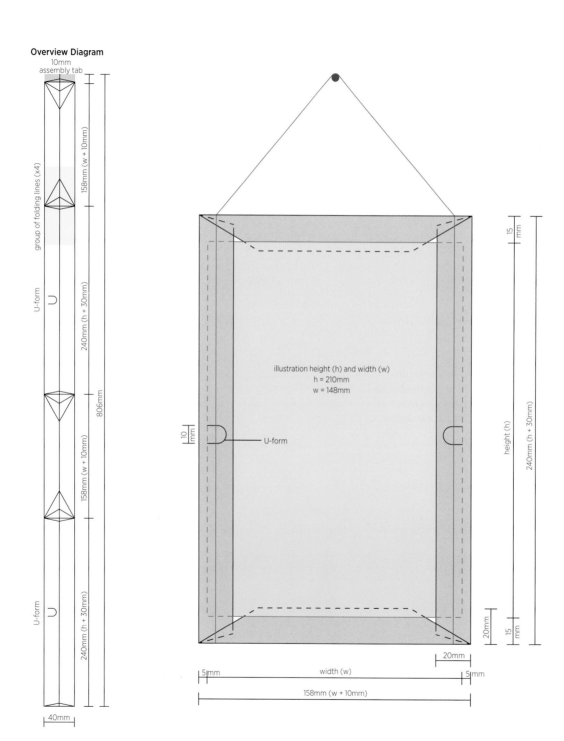

10mm
assembly tab

group of folding lines (x4)

158mm (w + 10mm)

U-form

240mm (h + 30mm)

806mm

158mm (w + 10mm)

U-form

240mm (h + 30mm)

40mm

illustration height (h) and width (w)
h = 210mm
w = 148mm

U-form

10 mm

15 mm

height (h)

240mm (h + 30mm)

20mm

15 mm

20mm

5 mm   width (w)   5 mm

158mm (w + 10mm)

Scoring

Score the central vertical line along the length of the paper strip (see Overview Diagram).

Referring to the measurements on the right-hand edge of the Overview Diagram (adapting these to the height and width measurements of your illustration as necessary), score horizontal lines at the positions indicated.

For each group of folding lines, refer to the measurements given in the Overview Diagram and the Group of Folding Lines Diagram to mark points A, B, C, D and E, then score all diagonal lines between the marked points as shown in the Group of Folding Lines Diagram. Each group of folding lines makes a corner of the picture frame.

The picture frame will be assembled at one of the corners, so it is necessary to mark points C, D and E at the bottom edge of the paper strip and to score diagonal lines between them (see Overview Diagram).

Carefully cut out the two U-forms seen in the Overview Diagram (these will help to keep the illustration in place within the picture frame); these should be positioned in the middle of the height of the picture frame, making sure that they are both situated in the same vertical scored section.

Apply double-sided tape to the 10mm section at the top edge of the scored paper (see Overview Diagram).

Folding

Pre-fold the central scored vertical line in both directions, then pre-fold the horizontal lines in both directions.

Fold the paper vertically along the central scored line.

Group of Folding Lines Diagram

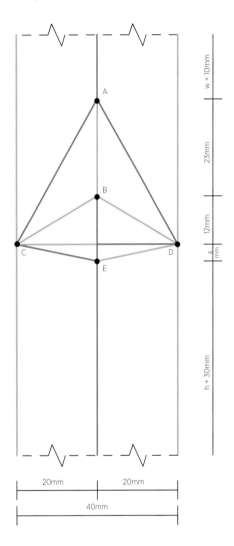

Choose your paper colour to accentuate your illustration, or make it in the same shade as your wall décor for a more neutral look.

Pleating Diagram

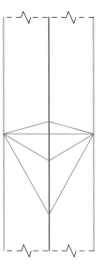

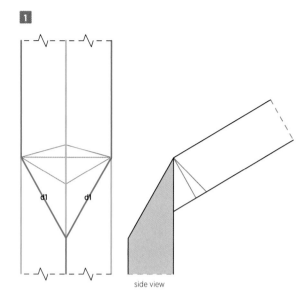

side view

Pre-fold all the diagonal scored lines in both directions.

Pleat paper along scored vertical lines of each segment as indicated on the Pleating Diagram (see Techniques: Folding, Pleating).

Now to fold the 90 degree corners that will clamp your picture in place. For each group of folding lines:

▷ Valley fold the two scored diagonal lines labelled d1 on Diagram 1.

▷ Mountain fold the two scored diagonal lines labelled d2 on Diagram 2.

▷ The final step in forming the corner requires that you manipulate the scored horizontal folds labelled h1 and h2 and the scored diagonal folds labelled d3 on Diagram 3 to bring the vertical sections of the paper together to make a 90 degree angle as shown in the 3D perspective (see Diagram 3).

Assembly

Remove the backing from the double-sided tape and attach the ends of the picture frame together, ensuring that the taped edge is on the reverse of the inner edge of the picture frame.

To put your illustration into the picture frame, place the frame right side down so that U-forms are facing you. Place the illustration right side down next to the frame and slide it in from the side, so that it slips under the corners. Centre the illustration and use the U-form 'clips' to secure it horizontally.

Take a 2 metre length of cord and loop it around the edge of the picture frame. Check the length required to hang from your picture hook, and tie the ends together with an overhand knot at that point, trimming off any excess. Your picture is now ready to hang.

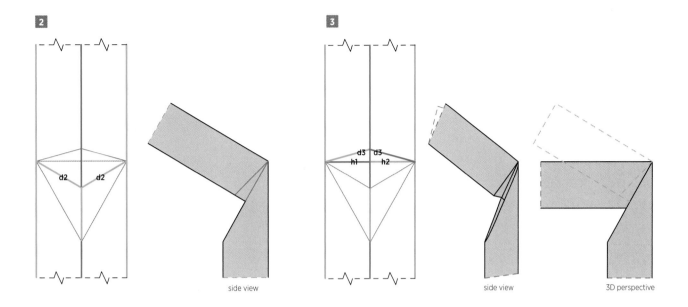

side view

side view   3D perspective

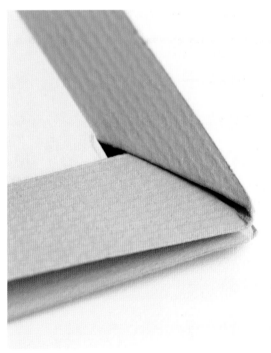

Window Decoration

We live in an old house that has small paned windows, which are ideal for hanging decorations from. Our design features a circular folded motif, with slits cut across the folds towards the outer edges, so that when the sun shines, the light makes patterns through the paper. The ornament reminds us of a meringue, an affect that was achieved by using curved rather than straight fold lines, and this will require a little more concentration.

YOU WILL NEED

- 1 piece of 210-270gsm paper, 190 x 190mm

If you are a beginner, try making the decoration with straight folds before moving on to the curved fold version.

Scoring

Make a copy of the template (see Templates) and fix it onto your paper with masking tape. Trace the outline of the template onto your paper, then score over the curved lines that run from the centre to the outer edge, pressing hard enough to impress the lines onto the paper.

Continue to score the two rounds of black curved lines, making sure to keep a distance of 4mm between the scored lines in each round as shown as in the Overview Diagram.

Remove the template from the paper. Carefully cut around the outer edge of the circle using scissors or a craft blade and use a 2mm hole punch to punch the hole (see Overview Diagram).

Overview Diagram

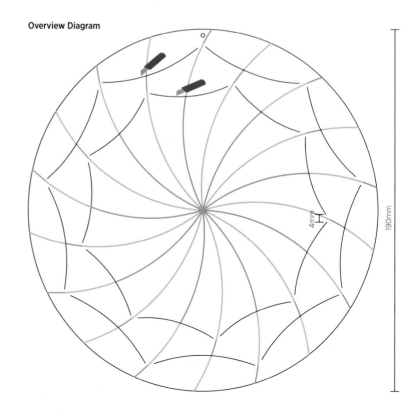

4mm

190mm

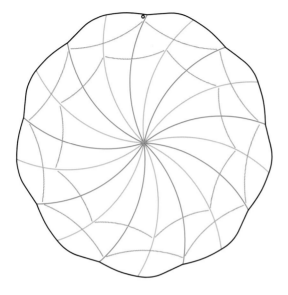

1

Folding

Pre-fold the scored curved lines that radiate from the centre, in both directions: this is easiest to do if you start folding from the outside edge and gently follow the curve towards the centre. Do not try to fold each line in one go, as you would a straight line, but follow the curve of the fold, pinching the paper between thumb and index finger, then releasing to move along the fold, before pinching again, and repeat until you have reached the end of the curved line.

Mountain fold the scored orange lines and valley fold the scored blue lines as shown on Diagram 1.

Cut the inner round of black scored curved lines as shown on the Overview Diagram and Diagram 2, taking care to keep the distance of 4mm between the ends of the cutting lines.

Change the direction of the scored curved folds between the inner round and the outer edge of the model as shown on Diagram 2.

Cut the outer round of black scored curved lines as shown on the Overview Diagram and Diagram 3, taking care to keep the distance of 4mm between the ends of the cutting lines.

Change the direction of the scored curved folds between the outer round and the outer edge of the model as shown on Diagram 3.

The decoration looks best if the centre of the model is a mountain; press at the centre point (labelled A in Diagram 3) as necessary to achieve this.

Assembly

To make a hanging loop, cut a 0.5m length of cord, fold it in half to make a loop and thread the loop through the hole at the top of the folded model (see Diagram 4). Adjust the length of the loop as required, then tie the ends together with an overhand knot (see Diagram 5).

2

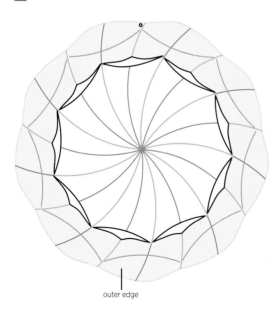

outer edge

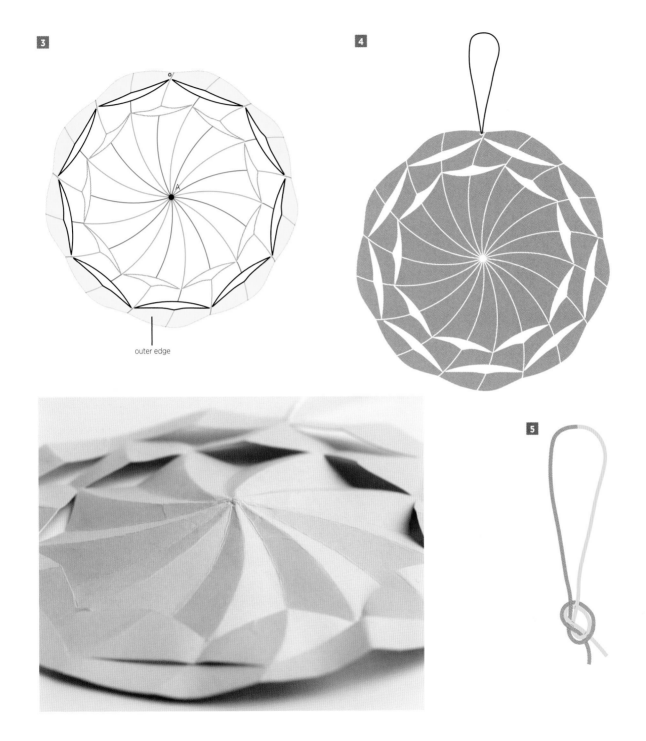

outer edge

String of Stars

A string of lights decorated with origami stars is a great way to bring an illuminated focus to a room at any time of year, so there's no need to pack these away with the rest of the Christmas decorations. Each ball shape is folded and formed to reveal a six-point star at its centre.

YOU WILL NEED

- 1 piece of 210-270gsm paper, 139 x 120mm, per star decoration
- LED string lights (see Techniques: Lamp Safety)

Scoring

Make a copy of the template (see Templates) and fix it temporarily onto a piece of your paper with masking tape. Trace the outline of the template and carefully cut out with a craft blade and a metal ruler.

Take one piece of paper and referring to the measurements on the Overview Diagram, score the horizontal lines.

Rotate the paper clockwise by 60 degrees, so that triangle A is now at the bottom left-hand corner, and score the horizontal lines as you did before.

Rotate the paper clockwise by 60 degrees one last time and score the remaining horizontal lines.

Cut out the hexagon shape in the centre and use a hole punch to punch the hole (see Overview Diagram) – a 2mm hole punch should be fine but check the widest diameter of the LED lights on the light string and make the hole just a little bit smaller than this.

Overview Diagram

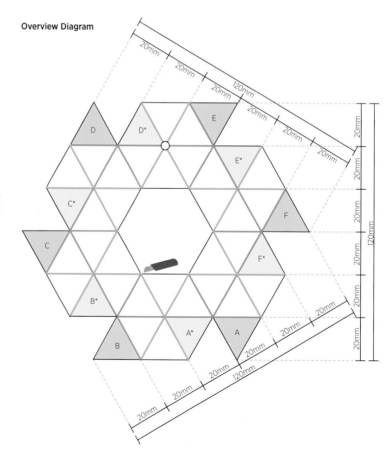

Folding

Fold all the scored lines in the direction as indicated in the Overview Diagram.

Glue triangle surface A to the reverse side of surface A*, and repeat to glue B to B*, C to C*, D to D*, E to E*, and F to F* (see Diagram 1). Your completed star model will now look like that shown in Diagram 2.

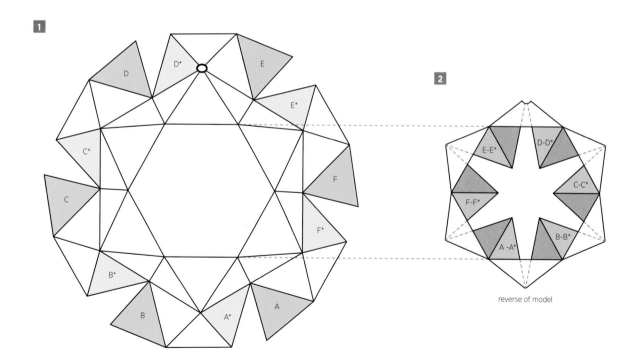

reverse of model

Assembly

Once you have made the necessary number of stars, attach them to your light string by pushing one of the LED lights through a hole on each of the decorations (see Diagram 3).

Alternatively, to hang the stars as individual decorations, take a length of cord, fold it in half to make a loop and tie the ends with an overhand knot. Thread the loop through the hole, so that the knot is on the inside of the model just below the hole (see Diagram 4).

Faux Ceramic Clock

This striking design is not only a beautiful piece of wall art, but also a functional clock suitable for any room in your home. The circular pattern features individual segments to represent the 12 numbers on a clock face. Make the clock to match your existing decor or choose a contrasting colour to create a bold feature. Using a pale coloured paper, however, will ensure that the folds are all clearly visible.

YOU WILL NEED

- 1 piece of 210-270gsm paper, 970 x 150mm
- 1 piece of 340gsm cardstock, 300 x 300mm
- An analogue clock mechanism with a spindle length of 31mm (see Suppliers)
- A minute hand around 120mm and an hour hand around 90mm (see Suppliers)

Scoring

Score vertical lines at intervals of 20mm along the length of the piece of paper (see Overview Diagram). There will be a 10mm section remaining on the right-hand edge, which will become an assembly tab. Each set of four 20mm scored sections forms a segment (see Segment Diagram).

Starting with the first segment, referring to the measurements given in the Segment Diagram, mark points A, B, C, D, E, F and G, then score diagonal lines between the marked points as shown (see Segment Diagram). Repeat for each segment and continue to partially mark and score lines across the assembly tab section (see Overview Diagram).

Apply double-sided tape to the 10mm section on the right-hand edge of the scored piece (see Overview Diagram). Cut the corners of the assembly tab at a 45 degree angle.

Use a 2mm hole punch to punch holes 10mm in from the side and bottom edges in each 20mm scored section (see Overview Diagram and Segment Diagram).

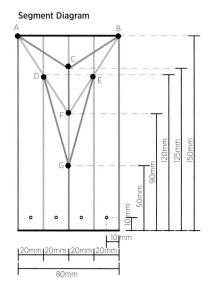

Segment Diagram

Overview Diagram

segment (x12)

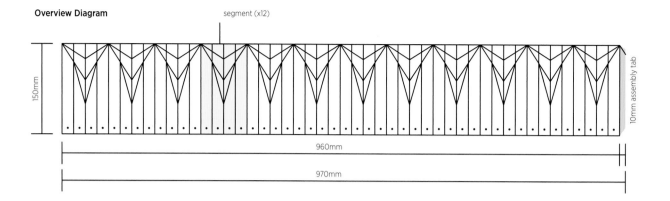

150mm

960mm

970mm

10mm assembly tab

Pleating Diagram

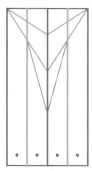

Folding

Pre-fold each of the scored vertical lines in both directions.

Fold the paper vertically along the central scored line of the first segment. Pre-fold all the diagonal scored lines of the segment in both directions. Repeat for remaining segments.

Pleat paper along scored vertical lines of each segment as indicated on the Pleating Diagram (see Techniques: Folding, Pleating).

Starting with the first segment, and referring to Techniques: Changing Direction, mountain fold the central two scored diagonal lines (labelled d1 on Diagram 1). Repeat for remaining segments.

Valley fold the top two scored diagonal lines (labelled d2 on Diagram 2). Repeat for remaining segments.

Valley fold the bottom two scored diagonal lines (labelled d3 on Diagram 3). Repeat for remaining segments.

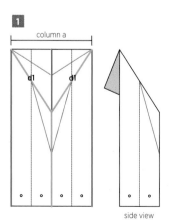

column a

d1   d1

side view

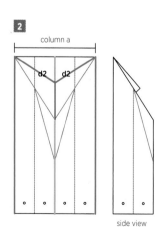

column a

d2   d2

side view

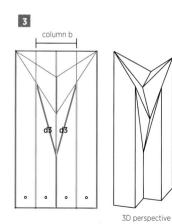

column b

d3   d3

3D perspective

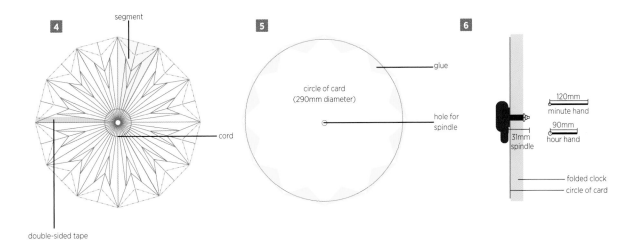

4 segment — cord — double-sided tape

5 glue — circle of card (290mm diameter) — hole for spindle

6 120mm minute hand — 90mm hour hand — 31mm spindle — folded clock — circle of card

Assembly

Remove the backing from the double-sided tape at the end of the folded piece and attach the ends of the model together to create a tube, ensuring that the taped edge is on the reverse of the clock.

Thread a 1 metre length of cord through the holes along the bottom of the folded piece. Pull the cord to create a circular shape and secure the ends of the cord by tying a sliding knot (see Techniques: Sliding Knot). Gently pull the cord to tighten and flatten the clock (see Diagram 4). To keep the clock shape secured, make a third knot close to knot 2, then trim off the remaining cord length.

> *Ensure that your sliding knot is on the reverse of the clock for a neat, professional finish.*

Cut a 290mm circle from the 340gsm cardstock. Make a small hole in the centre for the spindle. Glue the outer triangular shapes on the clock to the card circle (see shaded areas on Diagram 5).

Assemble the clock mechanism by placing the spindle through the hole in the centre of the folded clock. Use the screw provided to secure the mechanism in place, and attach the minute and hour hands to finish (see Diagram 6).

> *The spindle length must be 31mm to ensure that the clock mechanism will fit correctly. You can also add a second hand if desired.*

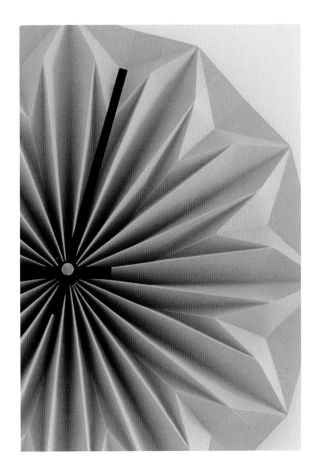

Modular Wall Art

The exciting thing about modular wall art is that no two finished pieces need to be the same, as the individual units can be combined in many ways. We used a hexagon shape as the basis for our pattern, exploring depth and dimension as we developed the design. Each module requires just one small piece of paper, so you can get creative with colour. We chose an ombré effect in blue, but you could fold a rainbow.

YOU WILL NEED

- 19 pieces of 210-270gsm paper, 139 x 120mm

You can change the shape of your finished model, making it with fewer or more modules, and the number of pieces of paper you require will depend on the number of units you choose to make.

Scoring

For each module (make 19 for the model shown):

▷ Make a copy of the template (see Templates) and fix it temporarily onto your paper with masking tape. Trace the outline of the template and carefully cut out with a craft blade and a metal ruler.

▷ Orientate the cut out hexagon shape so that there is a point at the top and the bottom. Referring to the measurements given on the Overview Diagram, mark and score vertical lines, using the corners of your cut out shape to help you.

▷ Rotate the paper clockwise by 60 degrees, so that triangles C* and C are now the bottom point and mark and score the vertical lines as before.

Overview Diagram

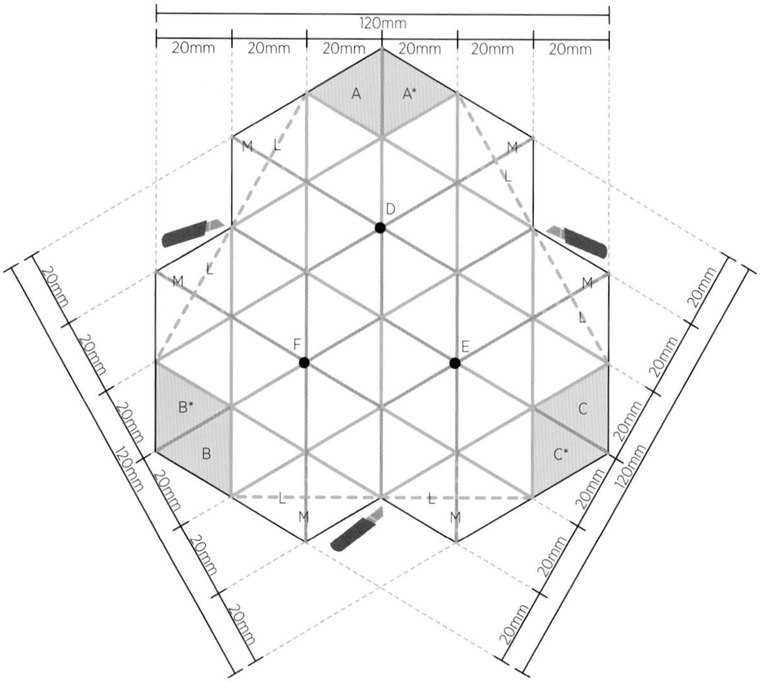

▷ Rotate the paper clockwise by 60 degrees one last time and score the remaining vertical lines.

▷ Use a craft blade and a metal ruler to cut out the triangles from the three areas marked with a blade symbol on the Overview Diagram.

▷ Score the dashed lines labelled L on the Overview Diagram.

Folding

For each module:

▷ Pre-fold all the scored lines in both directions.

▷ Mountain fold the dashed lines labelled L on the Overview Diagram.

▷ Valley fold the blue lines between A and A* , B and B*, C and C* and glue the sides together. Turn the model over to the reverse side – it should look like Diagram 1. Take care that the rest of the model does not fold yet.

▷ Turn the model over to the front side as in Diagram 2. Press point D downwards to create the mountain and valley folds of hexagon 1 (see Diagram 3). Repeat for points E and F to create the mountain and valley folds of hexagon 2 and 3. Valley fold lines G, H and I (see Diagram 3).

▷ Turn the model over to the reverse side once again, and fold the glued triangles sideways so they touch the inside of the model.

Assembly

Once you have made all your modular pieces, you can fit them together with glue, either following our layout or in a pattern of your own design. Put glue on sides J* and K* on one module and attach to sides J and K on another module (see Diagram 4 to see how the modules start to come together). The easiest way to start is to attach three modules together and add more from there.

After you have finished attaching the modules, turn the model over to the reverse side to complete the folding work. Where three modules come together, valley fold lines M as on Diagram 5 so that a hexagon shape forms in this location.

On the outer edges of the finished model, mountain fold lines L as on Diagram 5, bringing the sides completely together. The model will have a curved shape, and it can stand on a shelf or be hung on the wall.

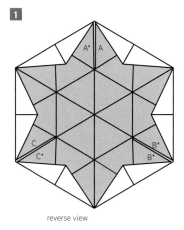

reverse view

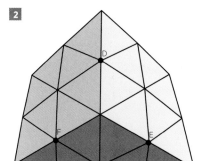

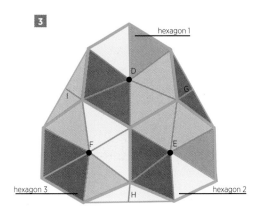

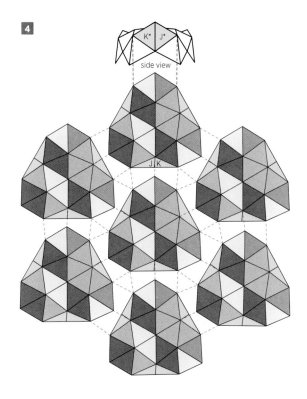

side view

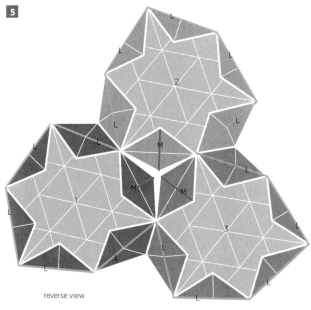

reverse view

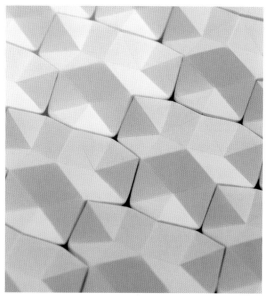

Experiment with making a larger number of modules to create large dome shapes.

Waves Picture

This origami picture was inspired by our love of the sea and the repeating pattern of the folds reminds us of breaking waves. As it is quite challenging to fold such a detailed texture over a large piece of paper, we have broken it down into five smaller pieces, using two pieces of white for the top of the wave with gradations of blue for the three remaining sections. What colour combination will you choose?

YOU WILL NEED

- 5 pieces of 210-270gsm paper, 360 x 112.5mm
- Picture frame, 500 x 700mm

Scoring

Score vertical lines at alternating intervals of 15mm and 45mm (see Segment Diagram X) along the length of each of the five pieces of paper (see Overview Diagram).

Take one piece of paper and, starting with the first segment and referring to the measurements given in the Segment Diagram, mark points A, B, C, D, E, F, G, H, I, J, K and L, then score diagonal lines between the marked points as shown (see Segment Diagram). Repeat for each segment.

Repeat to mark points and score diagonal lines between marked points on the remaining four pieces of paper.

Referring to the Overview Diagram, apply 6mm double-sided tape to run neatly along the top scored line on four of the five pieces of paper, as marked a, b, c and d.

Segment Diagram X

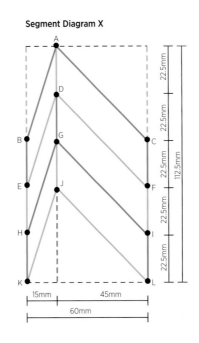

Segment Diagram Y

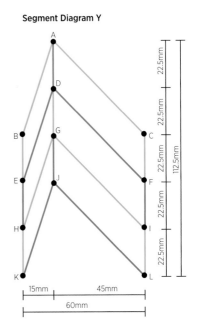

Overview Diagram

X 112.5mm

Y 112.5mm

X 112.5mm

Y 112.5mm

X 112.5mm

6mm assembly tab

360mm

Referring to the Overview Diagram, notice that three of the papers are labelled as Row X and two are labelled Row Y; please note that Row X is different for each of the three papers. The three different shapes are indicated in the Overview Diagram and with dashed lines in Segment Diagram X.

Cut each of the five pieces of paper so that they appear as in the Overview Diagram, referring to the measurements given in the Overview Diagram and the Segment Diagrams to guide you.

Folding

There are three papers that have the same shape. Make sure to use two of these as Row Y papers and one as a Row X paper. For each piece of paper, pre-fold each of the scored vertical lines in both directions and pleat as follows:

▷ For Row X papers, as indicated on Pleating Diagram X (see Techniques: Folding, Pleating).

▷ For Row Y papers, as indicated on Pleating Diagram Y.

Now fold the diagonal lines. This is a bit of a challenge because, as the pleats are not symmetrical and will not overlap when the paper is folded along a vertical line, it is not possible to pre-fold the diagonals. Rather than the usual practice of bringing the sides of the fold together completely, you'll need to bring the sides of the fold together halfway to gently shape the paper.

▷ Fold the diagonal lines for Row X papers as shown on Diagram 1 (see note).

▷ Fold the diagonal lines for Row Y papers as shown on Diagram 2 (see note).

Note

Start folding the scored lines to the left, right, top and bottom edges of the paper; as the paper slowly starts to take on its shape, it will be possible to fold the diagonal lines towards the centre of the paper (see Diagrams 1 and 2 for 3D perspectives). Bring the sides of the diagonal folds together as much as possible by gently pushing together the vertical lines (1-2), (3-4), (5-6), (7-8), (9-10) and (11-12) as shown in Diagram 3; this sharpens the folds so that you get the desired depth to the paper.

Assembly

Working on one row at a time, remove the backing from the double-sided tape and attach it to its neighbouring row, aligning a to a*, b to b*, c to c* and d to d* (see Overview Diagram), ensuring that the taped edges are on the reverse.

Pleating Diagram X

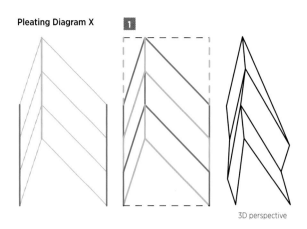

3D perspective

Pleating Diagram Y

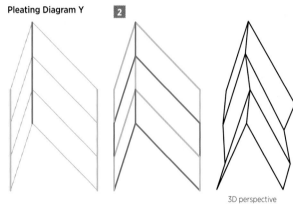

3D perspective

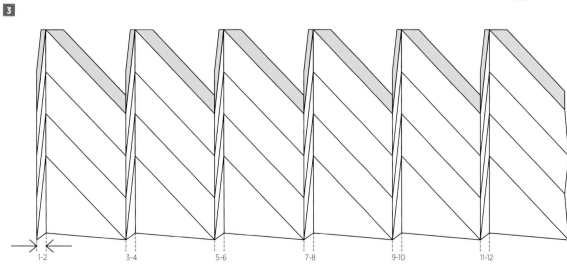

Decorative Mirror

This elegant mirror seems to defy the laws of physics – how can a delicate paper border secure the heavy mirrored glass? It is simply a clever illusion as although the origami triangles appear to clasp the mirror in place, a hidden split batten fixture attaches it directly to the wall, and the circular origami backing into which the mirror is slipped is hidden from view to leave only the decorative edge visible.

YOU WILL NEED

- 2 pieces of 210-270gsm paper, 1 piece 685 x 270mm and 1 piece 640 x 270mm
- Circular mirror, 300mm diameter and 5mm thick (see Suppliers)
- Split batten with distance to wall of 15mm (see Suppliers)
- Mirror fixing tape (see Suppliers)

Scoring

For each piece of paper:

▷ Score vertical lines along the length of the paper (see Overview Diagram) to the measurements given at the base of the Segment Diagram. Each segment measures 45mm wide and has a set of two partially scored 7.5mm sections (labelled column a) and two fully scored 15mm sections (labelled column b) (see Segment Diagram). There will be a 10mm section remaining on the right-hand edge, which will become an assembly tab.

▷ Score the four horizontal lines that run across the full paper width (see Overview Diagram), referring to the measurements given on the Segment Diagram.

▷ In each segment, cut out the 5mm rectangle shape in column b (see knife symbol on Segment Diagram).

▷ Referring to the measurements given on the Segment Diagram, mark points A, B, C, D, E, F, G, H and I in column b and points J, K and L in column a, then score diagonal lines between the marked points as shown (see Segment Diagram). Repeat for each segment and continue to partially mark and score lines across the assembly tab section (see Overview Diagram).

▷ Apply double-sided tape to the 10mm section on the right-hand edge of the scored piece (see Overview Diagram). Cut the corners of the assembly tab at a 45 degree angle.

▷ Use a 2mm hole punch to punch holes 7.5mm in from the side and bottom edges in each 15mm scored section (see Overview Diagram and Segment Diagram).

The space behind the lipped edge of the origami model could house a LED light string but you'll need to choose a pale coloured paper to let the light shine through.

Overview Diagram

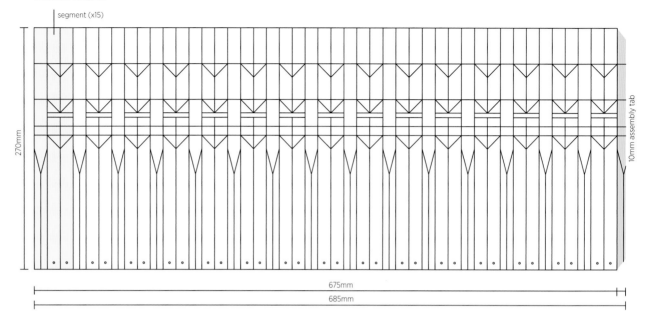

segment (x15)

270mm

10mm assembly tab

675mm

685mm

Note: your second piece of paper measures 640 x 270mm and therefore will have just 14 segments, making a total of 29 segments across the two pieces of paper.

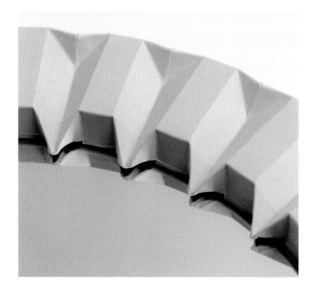

Folding

For each piece of paper:

▷ Pre-fold each of the scored vertical and horizontal lines in both directions: note that not all the vertical lines extend to the full height of the paper.

In the first segment on one of the pieces of paper:

▷ Fold the paper vertically along the central scored line between the two 7.5mm sections (note that this vertical line does not extend to the full height of the paper) and pre-fold the diagonal scored lines in this section in both directions.

▷ Fold the paper vertically along the central scored line between the two 15mm sections and pre-fold all the diagonal scored lines in this section in both directions.

Segment Diagram

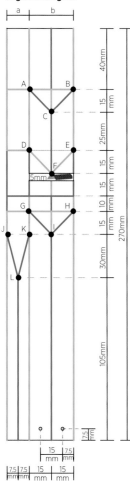

Pleating Diagram

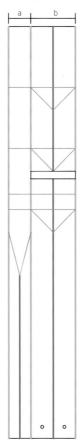

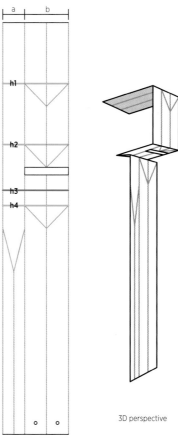

3D perspective

Repeat for the remaining segments on the first piece of paper, before replicating on the second piece of paper.

Pleat paper along scored vertical lines of each segment as indicated on the Pleating Diagram (see Techniques: Folding, Pleating): note again that not all the vertical lines extend to the full height of the paper.

Working on each piece of paper in turn and folding across the full width of the paper:

▷ Mountain fold the scored horizontal line labelled h1 on Diagram 1 over an angle of 90 degrees (i.e., fold along the edge of the table).

▷ Mountain fold the scored horizontal line labelled h2 on Diagram 1 over an angle of 90 degrees.

▷ Valley fold the scored horizontal line labelled h3 on Diagram 1 over an angle of 180 degrees (i.e., fold in half).

▷ Mountain fold the scored horizontal line labelled h4 on Diagram 1 over an angle of 90 degrees.

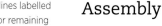

In the first segment on one of the pieces:

▷ Valley fold the two scored lines labelled d1 on Diagram 2 (refer to Techniques: Folding, Changing Direction). Repeat for remaining segments.

▷ Mountain fold the two scored lines labelled d2 on Diagram 2 by pushing down at the point marked X. Repeat for remaining segments.

▷ Valley fold the two scored lines labelled d3 on Diagram 2. Repeat for remaining segments.

▷ Valley fold the two scored lines labelled d4 on Diagram 3. Repeat for remaining segments.

Replicate on the second piece of paper.

Assembly

Remove the backing from the double-sided tape on the right-hand edge of one folded piece and attach to the left-hand edge of the other piece to create one long strip of folded paper.

Remove the backing from the double-sided tape on the right-hand edge of the second folded piece and attach the ends of the model together to begin to create the mirror frame shape.

Thread a 1 metre length of cord through the punched holes and gently pull the cord to close the back of the frame; secure the ends of the cord by tying a sliding knot (see Techniques: Sliding Knot). To keep the frame shape secured, make a third knot close to knot 2, then trim off the remaining cord.

Make a rectangular hole in the back of the origami model as indicated on Diagram 4; this should be the necessary size to accommodate the split batten fixture you are using.

Now you can insert the mirror into the origami frame. Place the folded model on a clean work surface. Gently place the mirror into the 5mm slots that you cut out of the paper at the start of the project.

Attach the split batten to the mirror with mirror fixing tape – this is very strong tape that can be used to attach metal parts to a mirror – by pressing the mirror and the split batten firmly together. Attach the hanging system to your wall following the manufacturer's instructions and hang the mirror (see Diagram 5).

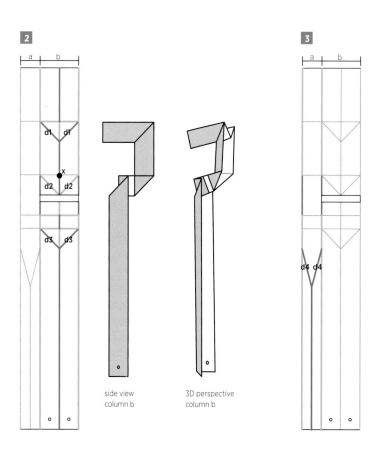

side view
column b

3D perspective
column b

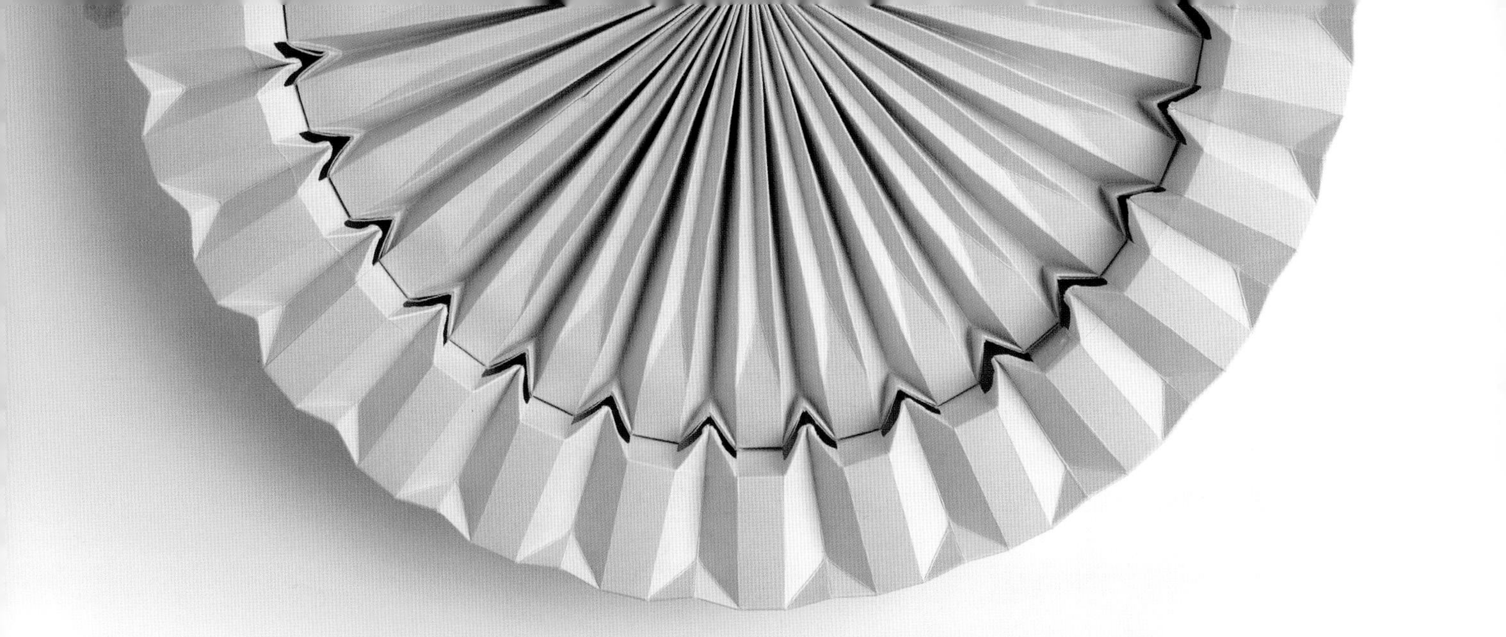

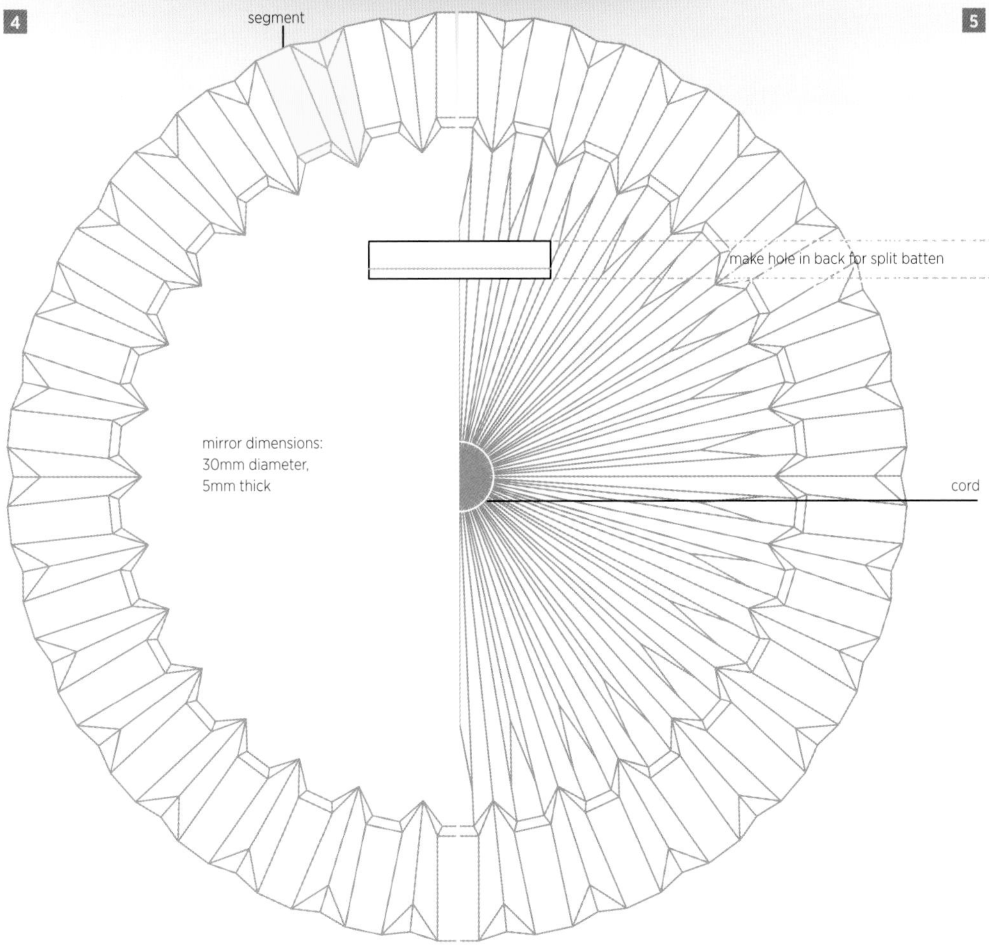
4
segment
make hole in back for split batten
mirror dimensions:
30mm diameter,
5mm thick
cord

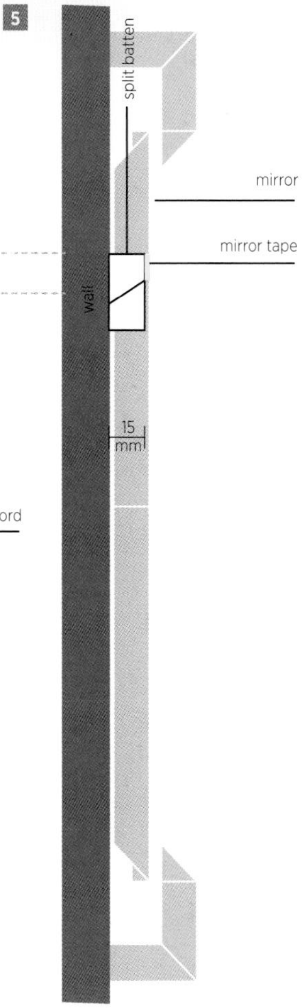
5
split batten
mirror
mirror tape
wall
15 mm

FOR THE CEILING

Leaf Mobile

This delightful decoration is inspired by autumn, when the leaves start to fall from the trees. It is a kinetic mobile, continuously searching for balance, often resulting in beautiful dynamic shadow play. The leaves are cut from relatively small pieces of paper and we used lots of different colours, although you could choose a more autumnal palette if you wish. Hang the leaves from white thread so they appear to dance in the air.

YOU WILL NEED

- 5 pieces of 210-270gsm paper, 140 x 170mm
- Combination pliers
- 0.9mm metal wire (see Suppliers)
- White thread, 5 metres

Scoring

To make each leaf, make a copy of the template (see Templates) and fix it onto your paper with masking tape. Trace the outline of the template onto your paper, then score the vertical line in the centre of the leaf, pressing hard enough to impress the line onto the paper. Score the inner leaf shape and each of the diagonal lines radiating out from the vertical line.

Remove the template from the paper. Use a craft blade and a metal ruler to cut through the diagonal lines radiating out from vertical line, cutting them through the scored vertical line, but stopping inside the scored inner leaf shape.

Carefully cut around the outer edge of the leaf using scissors or a craft blade and use a 2mm hole punch to punch the hole in the stalk (see Overview Diagram).

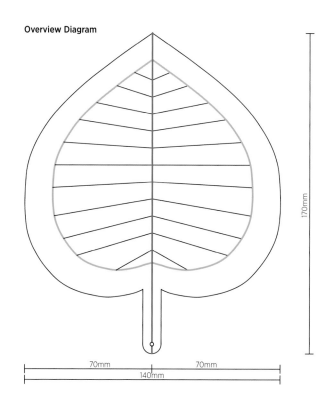

Overview Diagram

170mm

70mm   70mm

140mm

Folding

For each leaf, valley fold the blue vertical line and mountain fold the curved orange line as marked on the Overview Diagram. As you do so, the leaf shape will form. Make the folds sharper to create more depth in your leaf model.

Assembly

We have divided the assembly instructions into two parts: building the mobile, which gives an overview of the mobile building process; and mobile component assembly, which gives details of making and attaching the hanging arc components. The success of the mobile is all about finding the right balance, as seen in Diagram 1 and described in detail in Mobile Component Assembly.

Building the mobile

Cut five 500mm pieces of white thread. Attach a length of thread to each of the leaves and secure with two overhand knots.

Start with the leaf that hangs the lowest, labelled leaf 1 in Diagram 1, which together with leaf 2 hangs from arc A (refer to Mobile Component Assembly for making the arc).

Continue with arc B, from which the assembled arc A and leaf 3 hang (refer to Mobile Component Assembly for making the arc).

Continue with arc C, from which leaf 4 and leaf 5 hang (refer to Mobile Component Assembly for making the arc).

Finish with the widest arc D, from which joined arcs A and B, and arc C hang (refer to Mobile Component Assembly for making the arc).

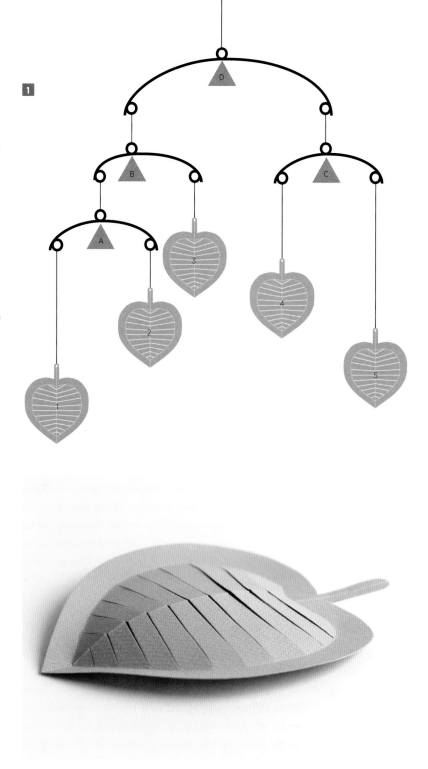

Mobile component assembly

Use combination pliers to cut four pieces of metal wire, three 300mm lengths for arcs A, B and C, and one 550mm length for arc D. Referring to the approximate measurements in Diagram 2, carefully bend the wire pieces with your hands to make the arcs.

When making the arcs, use masking tape to temporarily attach the elements that will hang from the arc that you are making (as seen in Diagram 1 and described in detail in Building the Mobile).

Find the balance point of a temporarily assembled arc by letting it find its balance on your fingertip. This may be in the centre, or slightly off-centre, or to the side. Clamp the combination pliers at the balance point, then remove the temporarily assembled parts from it.

Keeping your fingers close to the combination pliers, bend the arc 270 degrees clockwise. Release the pliers and clamp them back on at the top of the loop to complete the bending of the arc, forming a neat circle. Form the hanging loops at each end of the arc in the same way.

Reattach the elements that will hang from the arc that you have made, then attach a length of thread to the finished arc from which it will hang.

The type of wire sold in hobby shops is an easy thickness to work with. Practise making loops first.

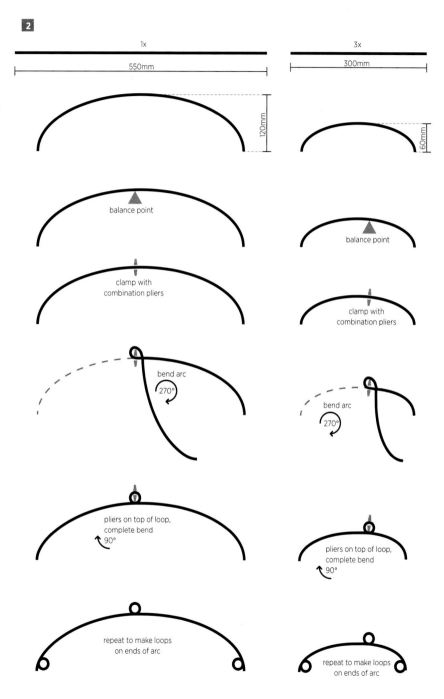

Ceiling Rose

This attractive ceiling ornament has been inspired by the traditional decorative features once found in older houses and now so often lost. This minimalistic design, based on a pleated paper sheet, looks fantastic in a modern setting and is functional too, attractively covering your ceiling connection. We made ours in white, to blend in with the ceiling colour, choosing a coloured cord for contrast.

YOU WILL NEED

- 1 piece of 150-190gsm paper, 970 x 180mm
- Cordset with bulb socket and LED light bulb (see Techniques: Lamp Safety)
- Flat plastic nylon washer with an inner diameter of 5mm

Scoring

Score vertical lines at intervals of 15mm along the length of the paper (see Overview Diagram). There will be a 10mm section remaining on the right-hand edge, which will become an assembly tab. Each set of two 15mm scored sections forms a segment (see Segment Diagram).

Starting with the first segment, referring to the measurements given in the Segment Diagram, mark points A, B, C, D, E and F, then score diagonal lines between the marked points as shown (see Segment Diagram). Repeat for each segment and continue to partially mark and score lines across the assembly tab section (see Overview Diagram).

Apply double-sided tape to the 10mm section on the right-hand edge of the paper (see Overview Diagram). Cut the corners of the assembly tab at a 45 degree angle.

Use a 4mm hole punch to punch holes 7.5mm in from the side and bottom edges in each 15mm scored section (see Overview Diagram and Segment Diagram).

> *For safety's sake it is important to use a plastic or metal ceiling cup beneath your paper ceiling rose, adapting the height of the origami as necessary.*

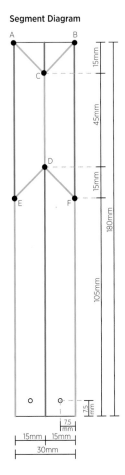

Segment Diagram

Overview Diagram

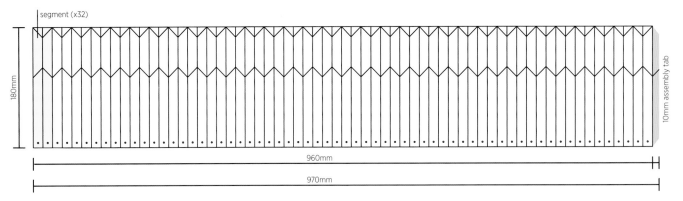

segment (x32)

180mm

10mm assembly tab

960mm

970mm

Pleating Diagram

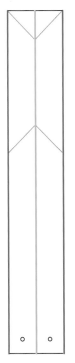

1

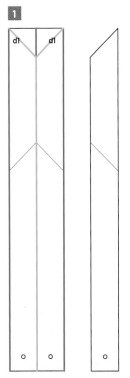

d1   d1

side view

2

d2   d2

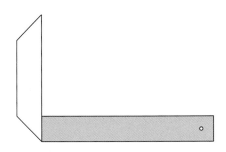

side view

Folding

Pre-fold each of the scored vertical lines in both directions.

Fold the paper vertically along the central scored line of the first segment. Pre-fold the diagonal scored lines of the segment in both directions. Repeat for remaining segments.

Pleat paper along scored vertical lines of each segment as indicated on the Pleating Diagram (see Techniques: Folding, Pleating).

Starting with the first segment and referring to Techniques: Folding, Changing Direction, mountain fold the two scored diagonal lines labelled d1 on Diagram 1. Repeat this process for remaining segments.

Starting with the first segment, mountain fold the two scored diagonal lines labelled d2 on Diagram 2. Repeat this process for remaining segments.

Assembly

It is important to read the safety instructions before installing the ceiling rose (see Techniques: Lamp Safety). Remember, you must use a plastic or metal ceiling cup beneath the paper ceiling rose, which should be used for decoration only.

To assemble your ceiling rose, remove the backing from the double-sided tape at the end of the folded piece of paper and attach the ends of the model together to create the ceiling rose shape, ensuring that the taped edge is on the reverse of the model.

Next thread a 1 metre length of cord through the punched holes and gently pull the cord to partially close. Then secure the cord ends by tying a sliding knot (see Techniques: Sliding Knot).

Place the paper ceiling rose over the light bulb socket and slide it up the electric cord until it touches the ceiling, covering the plastic or metal cup. Gently pull the cord to close the paper ceiling rose around the electric cord, storing the cord inside the model. To prevent the paper ceiling rose from sliding down, fit the plastic nylon washer: make a cut on one side to create an opening and clip the washer around the electric cord just below your folded model (see Diagram 3).

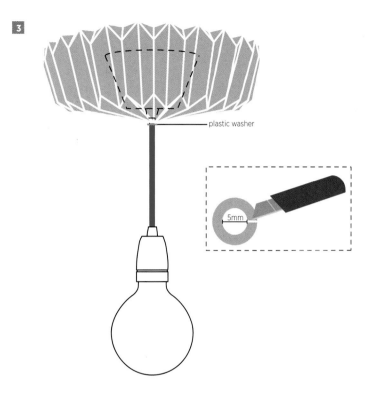

plastic washer

5mm

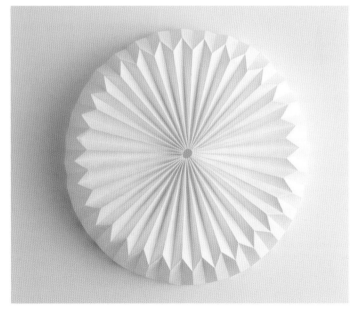

Pendant Lamp

This minimalist pendant lamp is just an electric cord with a light bulb socket attached to it, but our origami cover adds detail and texture and conceals the light bulb housing. The folds are very small and need to be precisely formed. You can open and close the folds at the top to easily install the cover onto your light bulb socket.

YOU WILL NEED

- 1 piece of 150-190gsm paper, 222 x 115mm
- Cordset with bulb socket measuring max. diameter of 50mm at widest point and LED light bulb (see Techniques: Lamp Safety)

Scoring

Score vertical lines at intervals of 6mm along the length of the paper (see Overview Diagram). There will be a 6mm section remaining on the right-hand edge, which will become an assembly tab. Each set of two 6mm scored sections forms a segment (see Segment Diagram).

Score the horizontal line that runs across the whole width of the paper 5mm from the bottom edge (see Overview Diagram).

Starting with the first segment, referring to the measurements given in the Segment

Diagram, mark points A, B, C, D, E and F, then score diagonal lines between the marked points as shown (see Segment Diagram). Repeat for each segment and continue to partially mark and score lines across the assembly tab section (see Overview Diagram).

Apply double-sided tape to the 6mm section on the right-hand edge of the paper (see Overview Diagram). Cut the corners of the assembly tab at a 45 degree angle.

The instructions are designed to fit a bulb socket with a diameter of no more than 50mm at the widest point. If your bulb socket is larger, you will need to scale the pattern.

Segment Diagram

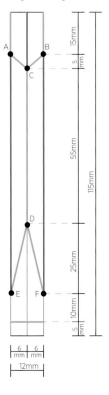

Overview Diagram

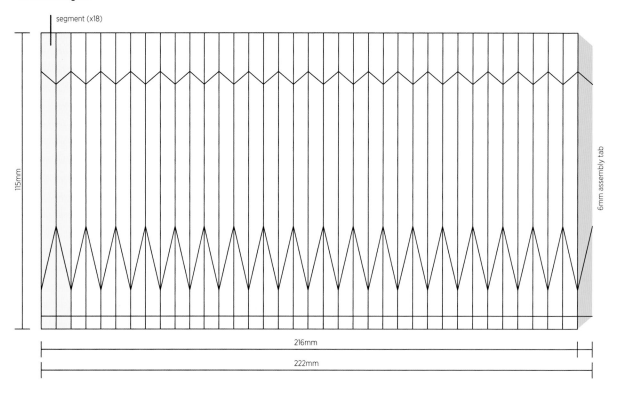

segment (x18)

115mm

6mm assembly tab

216mm

222mm

Folding

Pre-fold each of the scored vertical lines in both directions.

Pre-fold the horizontal line in both directions.

Fold the paper vertically along the central scored line of the first segment. Pre-fold the diagonal scored lines of the segment in both directions. Repeat for remaining segments.

Pleat paper along scored vertical lines of each segment as indicated on the Pleating Diagram (see Techniques: Folding, Pleating).

Starting with the first segment and referring to Techniques: Folding, Changing Direction, mountain fold the two scored diagonal lines labelled d1 on Diagram 1. Repeat for remaining segments.

Mountain fold the two scored diagonal lines labelled d2 on Diagram 2. Repeat for remaining segments.

Mountain fold the scored horizontal line labelled h1 on Diagram 3 across the whole width of the paper, bringing the sides of the fold completely together to give a double layer of paper along the bottom edge of your socket cover. Note that the area below the diagonal lines d1 will become flat when you do this.

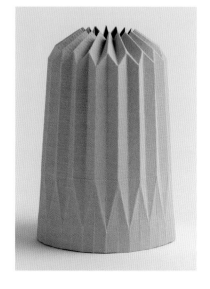

Assembly

It is important to read the safety instructions before installing the paper bulb socket cover (see Techniques: Lamp Safety), and to make sure that the power to the socket is switched off.

To assemble your bulb socket cover, remove the backing from the double-sided tape at the end of the folded piece of paper and attach the ends of the model together to create a tube, ensuring that the taped edge is on the reverse of the model.

Open the folds at the top of the paper socket cover to create an opening for the light bulb socket (make sure that the light bulb has been removed) and place the paper socket cover over the light bulb socket from below. Gently push the folds of the paper socket cover to close at the top (see Diagram 4). Fit an attractive looking light bulb into the light bulb socket and switch on the power again.

4

50mm

Pleating Diagram

1

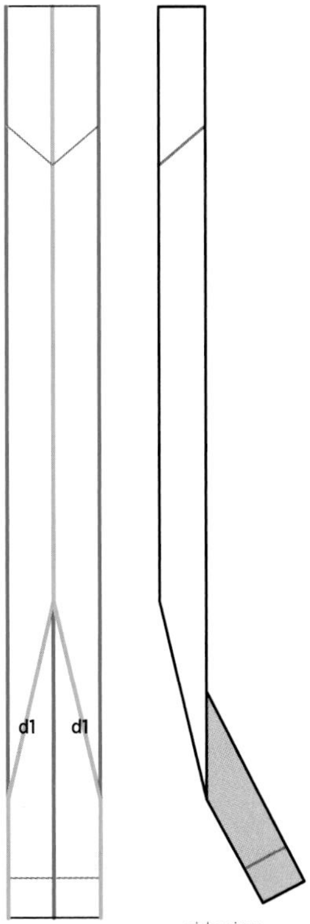

d1   d1

side view

2

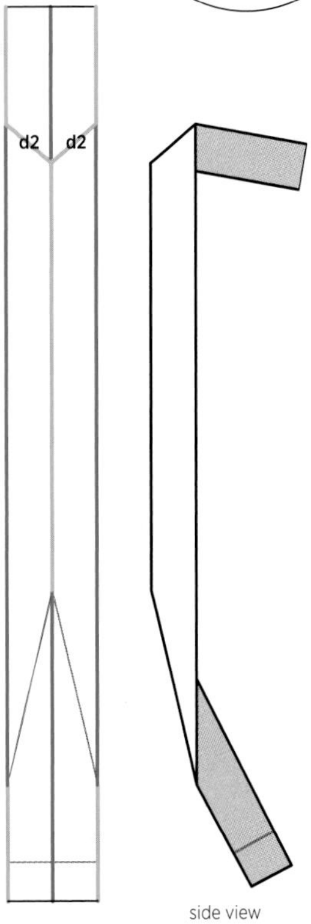

d2   d2

side view

3

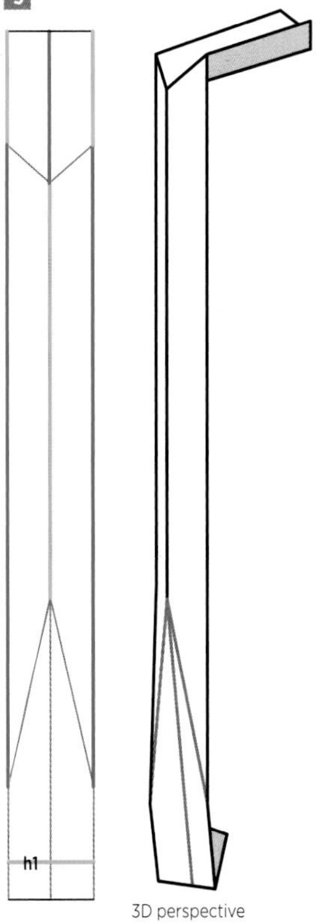

h1

3D perspective

Lampshade Diffuser

Recently we bought some very nice vintage ceiling lights made from metal and glass, but we missed the soft glow of light filtering through a paper shade. So we developed a minimalistic folding technique to make a white paper diffuser that can be adapted for any shade with a circular base. We converted one of our vintage lights to become a table lamp, but it could just as easily hang from the ceiling.

YOU WILL NEED

- 1 piece of 150-190gsm paper, size depends on the inner diameter of your lamp (see Calculating the Paper Size)
- Cordset with bulb socket and LED light bulb (see Techniques: Lamp Safety)
- Lampshade with a circular base

Scoring

Carefully cut out the paper to the size required using a craft blade and a metal ruler: in our example, our paper size is 406 x 103mm (see Calculating the Paper Size).

Score vertical lines at intervals of half of the segment width along the length of the paper (which in our example is 24.75mm). There will be a 10mm section remaining on the right-hand edge, which will become an assembly tab (see Overview Diagram). Each set of two scored sections forms a segment (see Segment Diagram).

Score a horizontal line across the full width of the paper 10mm from the bottom edge (from which the assembly tabs will be cut later, to attach the diffuser to the inside of the lamp).

Starting with the first segment, referring to the measurements given in the Segment Diagram as adapted for your own lamp, mark points A, B, C and D, then score diagonal lines between the marked points as shown (see Segment Diagram). Repeat for each segment and continue to partially mark and score lines across the assembly tab section (see Overview Diagram).

Apply double-sided tape to the 10mm section on the right-hand edge and bottom edge of the scored piece (see Overview Diagram). Make the assembly tabs at the bottom edge, extending the scored diagonal lines to the bottom edge of the paper to guide you, then cut out the triangles in between with a craft blade and metal ruler. Cut the corners of the assembly tab at the right-hand edge at a 45 degree angle.

Use a 2mm hole punch to punch holes at the halfway point between the scored vertical lines (at 12.4mm in our example) and 10mm in from top edge (see Overview Diagram and Segment Diagram).

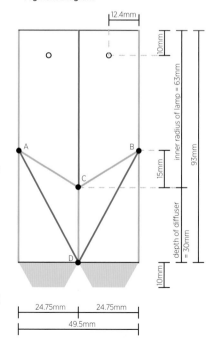

Segment Diagram

Overview Diagram

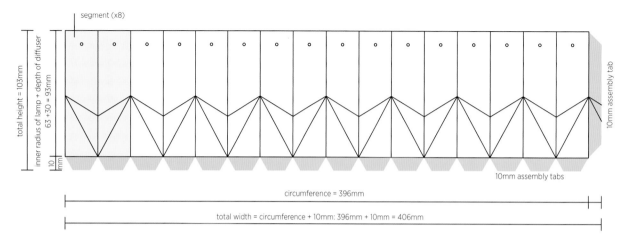

segment (x8)

total height = 103mm

inner radius of lamp + depth of diffuser
63 +30 = 93mm

10mm

10mm assembly tab

10mm assembly tabs

circumference = 396mm

total width = circumference + 10mm: 396mm + 10mm = 406mm

Pleating Diagram

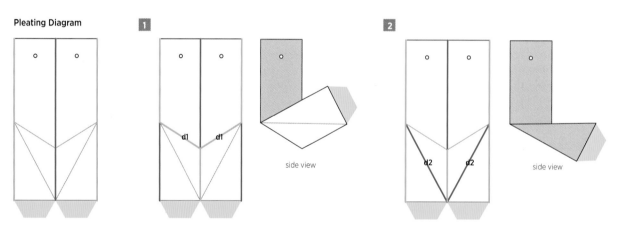

1

d1 d1

side view

2

d2 d2

side view

Folding

Pre-fold each of the scored vertical lines in both directions.

Pre-fold each of the scored horizontal lines for the assembly tabs at the bottom edge of the paper in both directions.

Fold the paper vertically along the central scored line of the first segment. Pre-fold the diagonal scored lines of the segment in both directions. Repeat this process for the remaining segments.

Pleat paper along scored vertical lines of each segment as indicated on the Pleating Diagram (see Techniques: Folding, Pleating).

Starting with the first segment and referring to Techniques: Folding, Changing Direction, mountain fold the two scored diagonal lines labelled d1 on Diagram 1. Repeat for the remaining segments.

Valley fold the two scored diagonal lines labelled d2 on Diagram 2. Repeat for the remaining segments.

Assembly

It is important to read the safety instructions in the Techniques section before you begin to install the lampshade (see Techniques: Lamp Safety).

Remove the backing from the double-sided tape at the right-hand edge of the folded piece and attach the ends of the model together to create the shape of the diffuser, ensuring that the taped edge is on the reverse.

Remove the backing from the double-sided tape on the assembly tabs and attach the diffuser to the inside edge of your lamp.

Thread a 1 metre length of cord through the holes of the folded piece. Gently pull the cord to close the hole in the middle of the diffuser and secure the ends of the cord by tying a sliding knot (see Techniques: Sliding Knot), and use the sliding knot to close the base of the diffuser completely, slipping the spare cord inside the diffuser. (You can use the cord to open and close the diffuser when you need to change the light bulb.)

Depending on the material your lamp is made from, a specialist glue may give a better fixing result than double-sided tape.

Calculating the paper size

The size of your paper will depend on the inner diameter of your lampshade or lamp, and the number of folded segments will be determined by this measurement too. Measure the diameter at the base of your lampshade, from inner edge to inner edge.

For our small vintage lamp, this measured 126mm. We will use this as an example for how to calculate required paper size.

To determine the paper width and number of segments

Use the calculations given below:

Circumference = 3.14 x inner diameter: Start by calculating the circumference of the base of the lamp. In our example, this calculation is 3.14 x 126mm = 396mm.

Amount of segments = circumference ÷ approximate width of segments: The approximate width of a segment for the diffuser design is 50mm, so to determine the number of folded segments required in our example, the calculation is 396mm ÷ 50mm = 7.92 segments, which is then rounded up to make 8 segments.

Exact width of a segment = circumference ÷ amount of segments: In our example, this calculation is 396mm ÷ 8 = 49.5mm, so the exact width of a segment for our lamp is 49.5mm, and the exact width of a half segment is 24.75mm (this will be important when scoring the vertical lines for the folding pattern as shown in the Segment Diagram).

Returning to the width of the paper, add 10mm for the assembly tab, so in our example the final calculation for the width of the paper is 396mm + 10mm = 406mm (see Overview Diagram).

To determine the paper height

Use the calculation given below:

Height = inner radius + diffuser depth: The inner radius is half the inner diameter, so for our example, this is ½ x 126mm = 63mm. You can choose what depth your diffuser will be: in our example, this is 30mm, so our height calculation is 63mm + 30mm = 93mm. To this, 10mm needs to be added for the assembly tabs, so in our example the final calculation for the height of the paper is 93mm + 10mm = 103mm (see Overview Diagram).

Wave Lampshade

The elegant form of the wave lampshade is created with minimal folding. The shaped paper panels are attached to a wooden ring, and they overlap each other like the slats of a window blind, intensifying the colour of the paper where they do so. This gives a beautiful effect both during the day and the night. We used paper that is coloured on the front and white on the reverse for best results.

YOU WILL NEED

- 18 pieces of 290-340gsm paper, 170 x 530mm
- Wooden ring with 400mm inner diameter (see Suppliers)
- Staple gun
- Cordset with bulb socket and LED light bulb (see Techniques: Lamp Safety)

Preparing the template

The template is made up of three parts which need to be joined to make the panel template (see Templates). Make a copy of each part and attach them with strong tape by overlapping the parts so that the cross marks on each align, following the order in Diagram 1.

The inner part of an embroidery hoop is the perfect thing for the wooden ring.

1

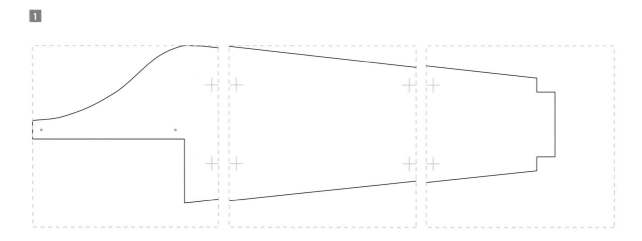

Segment Diagram

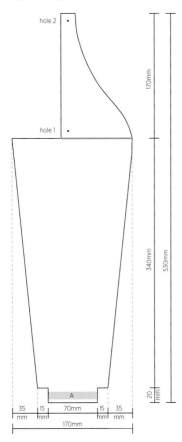

hole 2

hole 1

170mm

340mm

530mm

A

20 mm

35 mm | 15 mm | 70mm | 15 mm | 35 mm

170mm

You can glue a strip of canvas or paper to the inner edge of the wooden ring to hide the staples.

Scoring

Take one of your pieces of paper and place the joined panel template on top of it, fixing the template temporarily in place with masking tape. Trace around the outside edge of the template, then use a 2mm hole punch to punch the holes. (Note: if you have scaled the pattern, the diameter of the holes of the template will differ from that shown on the template, and you should just use the marked location of the holes to decide where to punch.)

Remove the template from the paper and carefully cut out with a craft blade, using a metal ruler for the straight edges.

Score the horizontal line beneath hole 1 (see Segment Diagram), using the cut out edge of the paper to guide you.

Apply 10mm double-sided tape to the tab (labelled A in the Segment Diagram).

Repeat for the remaining 17 pieces of paper.

Assembly

Working to fit one paper panel at a time, remove the backing from the double-sided tape at tab A and attach to the inner edge of the ring, making sure that the curved edge of the paper is on the left-hand side, and secure in place with the stapler gun. Put the staple at the location where the tabs overlap (see Diagram 2).

Work from right to left, going counter-clockwise around the ring so the papers overlap as in Diagram 2: the 18 paper panels will fit almost exactly along the inside.

On each paper panel, fold the scored horizontal line with a valley fold so the top part stands straight up.

Thread a 1 metre length of cord through the lower hole on each of the paper panels (labelled hole 1 on Segment Diagram). Gently pull the cord and secure the ends by tying a sliding knot (see Techniques: Sliding Knot).

Thread a 1 metre length of cord through the upper hole on each of the paper panels (labelled hole 2 on Segment Diagram). Gently pull the cord and secure as before.

Before installing the lampshade, it is important to read the safety instructions (see Techniques: Lamp Safety). Make sure that the power is switched off. Open the folds at the top of the lampshade to create an opening for the bulb socket. Place the lampshade over the socket from below (see Diagram 3). Gently pull both cords to close the lampshade at the top and create the wave shape. Fit a light bulb and switch on the power again.

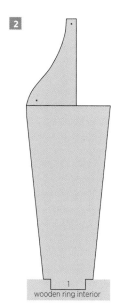
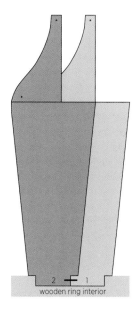
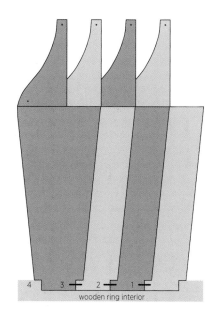

wooden ring interior

wooden ring interior

wooden ring interior

Scaling the pattern

The panel template can be scaled up or down for a wooden ring with a smaller or larger inner diameter, using the following formula to calculate the scaling factor:

Scaling factor = inner diameter of ring ÷ 400mm: for example, for a wooden ring with an inner diameter of 300mm, the calculation is 300mm ÷ 400mm = 0.75, to make a template that is three-quarters the original size.

To calculate the width of tab A, first calculate the circumference using the following formula:

Circumference = 3.14 x inner diameter: for example, for a wooden ring with an inner diameter of 300mm, the calculation is 3.14 x 300mm = 942mm.

Then complete the calculation for the width of tab A, using the following formula:

Width of tab A = circumference ÷ number of segments: for example, for a wooden ring with an inner diameter of 300mm, the calculation is 942mm ÷ 18 = 52.3mm.

The template parts should be scaled to the correct size before being joined as described in Preparing the Template.

Contemporary Lampshade

This stylish lampshade is extremely versatile, with its timeless and elegant shape. Varying the width of the pleats adds interest to the structure and creates definition between the sides. As the light bulb is fully enclosed inside the shade, it reduces the brightness to create a soft lighting effect. We have used white paper, as darker colours will allow less light through, but you could choose any pale or pastel tones.

YOU WILL NEED

- 2 pieces of 150-190gsm paper, 1000 x 700mm
- Cordset with bulb socket and LED light bulb (see Techniques: Lamp Safety)

Scoring

Starting at the left-hand edge of one of the pieces of paper, score a set of four vertical lines to form a segment, referring to the measurements at the base of the Segment Diagram (each segment measures 142mm wide).

Continue scoring vertical lines in this pattern to create seven scored segments (see Overview Diagram). There will be a 6mm section remaining on the right-hand edge, which will become an assembly tab.

Repeat with the other piece of paper to give you a total of 14 scored segments, seven per piece of paper.

Overview Diagram

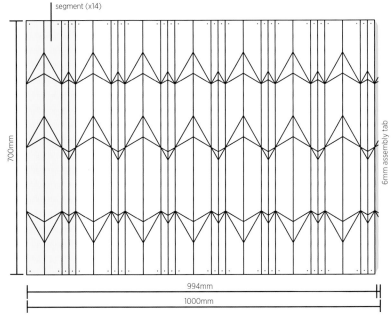

segment (x14)

700mm

6mm assembly tab

994mm

1000mm

Segment Diagram

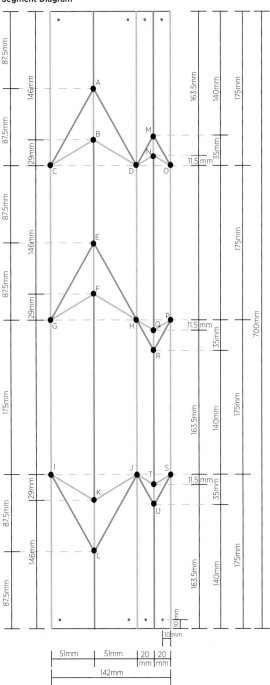

Starting with the first segment on each piece of paper, and referring to the measurements given on the left-hand side of the Segment Diagram, mark points A, B, C, D, E, F, G, H, I, J, K and L, then score diagonal lines between the marked points as shown (see Segment Diagram), continuing to partially mark and score lines across the assembly tab section (see Overview Diagram).

Referring to the measurements given on the right-hand side of the Segment Diagram, mark points M, N, O, P, Q, R, S, T and U, then score the remaining diagonal lines between the marked points as shown (see Segment Diagram).

Repeat for remaining segments.

Apply double-sided tape to the 6mm section on the right-hand edge of each piece of paper (see Overview Diagram). Cut the corners of the assembly tabs at a 45 degree angle.

Working first along the top edge of each piece of paper and then along the bottom edge, use a 4mm hole punch to punch holes in each segment as follows: 10mm in from the left-hand side and top/bottom edges for the first 51mm scored section; 10mm in from the right-hand side and top/bottom edges for the second 51mm scored section; and 10mm in from the side and top/bottom edges for each 20mm scored section (see Overview Diagram and Segment Diagram).

Pleating Diagram

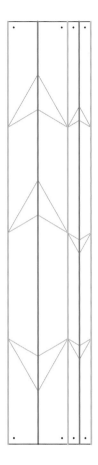

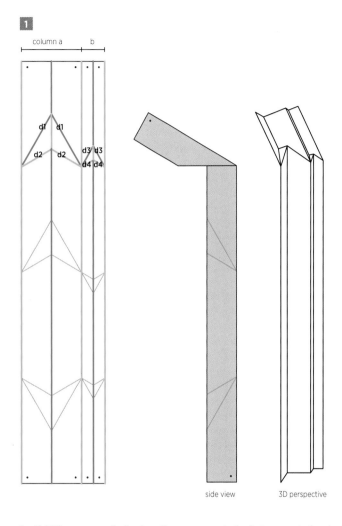

side view · 3D perspective

Folding

For each piece of paper, pre-fold each of the scored vertical lines in both directions.

In the first segment of each piece of paper:

▷ Fold the paper vertically along the central scored line between the two 51mm scored sections. Pre-fold the diagonal scored lines of the segment in both directions.

▷ Fold the paper vertically along the central scored line between the two 20mm scored sections. Pre-fold the diagonal scored lines of the segment in both directions.

Repeat for the remaining segments.

Pleat paper along scored vertical lines of each segment as indicated on the Pleating Diagram (see Techniques: Folding, Pleating).

In the first segment of each piece of paper and referring to Techniques: Folding, Changing Direction:

▷ Valley fold the two scored lines labelled d1 on Diagram 1 and mountain fold the two scored lines labelled d2 on Diagram 1.

▷ Valley fold the two scored lines labelled d3 on Diagram 1 and mountain fold the two scored lines labelled d4 on Diagram 1.

Repeat for the remaining segments.

In the first segment of each piece of paper:

▷ Valley fold the two scored lines labelled d5 on Diagram 2 and mountain fold the two scored lines labelled d6 on Diagram 2.

▷ Mountain fold the two scored lines labelled d7 on Diagram 2 and valley fold the two scored lines labelled d8 on Diagram 2.

Repeat for the remaining segments.

In the first segment of each piece of paper:

▷ Mountain fold the two scored lines labelled d9 on Diagram 3 and valley fold the two scored lines labelled d10 on Diagram 3.

▷ Mountain fold the two scored lines labelled d11 on Diagram 3 and valley fold the two scored lines labelled d12 on Diagram 3.

Repeat for the remaining segments.

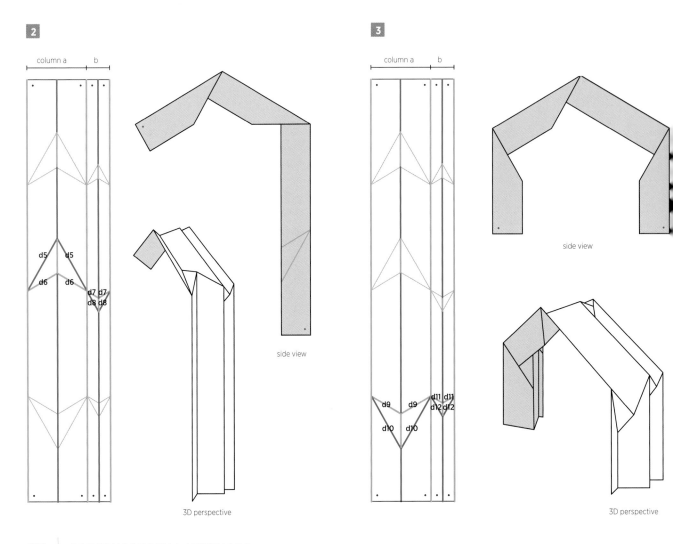

3D perspective

side view

3D perspective

Assembly

It is important to read the safety instructions in the Techniques section before you begin to install the lampshade (see Techniques: Lamp Safety).

Remove the backing from the double-sided tape on the right-hand edge of one folded piece and attach to the left-hand edge of the other piece to create one long strip of folded paper.

Remove the backing from the double-sided tape on the right-hand edge of the second folded piece and attach the ends of the model together to create a sphere, ensuring that the taped edge is on the reverse side.

Thread a 1 metre length of cord through the holes along the bottom of the folded piece and thread another 1 metre length of cord through the holes along the top of the folded piece. Pull both of the cords to make a spherical shape and secure the ends of the cord at the bottom of the lampshade by tying a sliding knot (see Techniques: Sliding Knot). Gently pull the cord at the bottom of the lampshade to tighten, and working only on this bottom edge, make a third knot close to knot 2, then trim off the remaining cord length (this will keep the sphere shape secured).

Place the cordset with bulb socket through the opening in the top of the lampshade. Secure the ends of the cord at the top of the lampshade by tying a sliding knot (see Techniques: Sliding Knot). Gently pull the cord at the top of the lampshade to tighten but don't trim off the remaining cord length as you will need to use this to be able to open the lampshade again to change the light bulb.

4

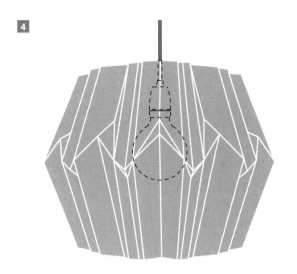

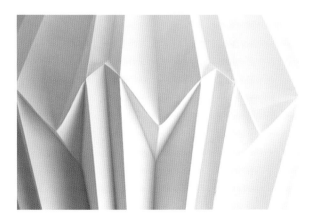

Moth Lampshade

This is our best-known design, sold in shops all over the world. We call it 'Moth' because we were inspired by the moths attracted to the artificial lights in our home. We make this shade in many sizes up to 700mm diameter, and here we share the instructions for making a 200mm diameter version. Choose white paper to let the light shine through or a dark colour as we have to direct the light downwards.

YOU WILL NEED

- 1 piece of 210-270gsm paper, 710 x 300mm
- Cordset with bulb socket and LED light bulb (see Techniques: Lamp Safety)

Scoring

Score vertical lines at intervals of 50mm along the length of the paper (see Overview Diagram). There will be a 10mm section remaining on the right-hand edge, which will become an assembly tab. Each set of two 50mm scored sections forms a segment (see Segment Diagram).

Score the two horizontal lines that run across the whole width of the paper.

Starting with the first segment, referring to the measurements given in the Segment Diagram, mark points A, B, C and D, then score diagonal lines between the marked points as shown (see Segment Diagram).

Overview Diagram

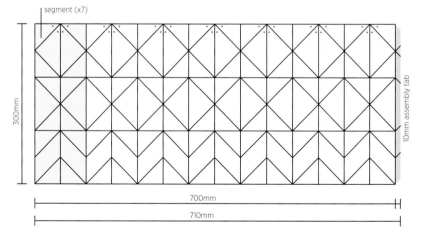

segment (x7)

300mm

10mm assembly tab

700mm

710mm

Segment Diagram

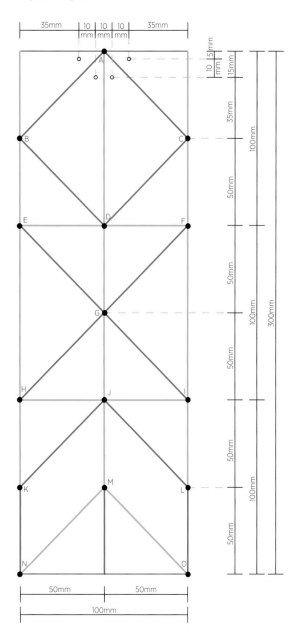

Mark points E, F, G, H and I, then score diagonal lines between the marked points as shown (see Segment Diagram).

Mark points J, K and L, then score diagonal lines between the marked points as shown (see Segment Diagram).

Mark points M, N, and O, then score diagonal lines between the marked points as shown (see Segment Diagram).

Repeat for remaining segments and continue to partially mark and score lines across the assembly tab section (see Overview Diagram).

Apply double-sided tape to the 10mm section on the right-hand edge of the scored piece of paper (see Overview Diagram). Cut the corners of the assembly tab at a 45 degree angle.

Use a 2mm hole punch to punch holes along the top of each 50mm scored section following the measurements given on the Segment Diagram.

Folding

Pre-fold each of the scored vertical lines and horizontal lines in both directions.

Fold the paper vertically along the central scored line of the first segment. Pre-fold the diagonal scored lines of the segment in both directions. Repeat for remaining segments.

Pleat the paper for each of the scored vertical lines of each segment as indicated on the Pleating Diagram (see Techniques: Folding, Pleating).

In the first segment and referring to Techniques: Folding, Changing Direction:

▷ Valley fold the two scored diagonal lines labelled d1 on Diagram 1.

▷ Mountain fold the scored horizontal line labelled h1 on Diagram 1 over an angle of 90 degrees (i.e., using the edge of the table to create the fold).

▷ Valley fold the two scored diagonal lines labelled d2 on Diagram 1.

Repeat for the remaining segments.

Pleating Diagram

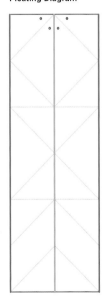

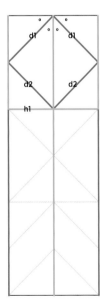

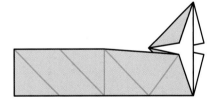

3D perspective

In the first segment and referring to Techniques: Folding, Changing Direction:

▷ Mountain fold the scored horizontal line labelled h2 on Diagram 2 over an angle of 90 degrees. Try to remove the pleat in the area between h1 and h2 to make this part of the paper into a flat square again.

▷ Next press point G downwards (see Diagram 2). As you do so you will create a slight valley fold in the two scored diagonal lines labelled d3 and the two scored diagonal lines labelled d4 (this almost happens by itself).

▷ Refold the valley fold on the two scored diagonal lines labelled d2 on Diagram 1 in order to be able to compress the segment up to the folded diagonal lines d3.

▷ Mountain fold the scored horizontal line labelled h2 on Diagram 2 over an angle of 180 degrees (i.e., fold in half).

▷ Valley fold the part of the central scored vertical line below h2 as in Diagram 2. You can now compress the complete segment.

Repeat for the remaining segments.

In the first segment:

▷ Try to remove the pleat in the area between h2 and the bottom edge to make this part of the paper into a flat square again.

▷ Valley fold the two scored diagonal lines labelled d5 on Diagram 3.

▷ Mountain fold the scored diagonal lines labelled d6 on Diagram 3.

Repeat for the remaining segments.

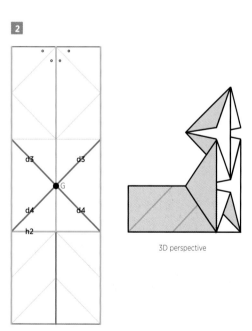

2

d3 d3

d4 d4

h2

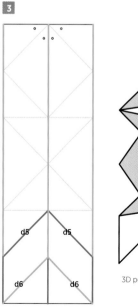

3D perspective

3

d5 d5

d6 d6

3D perspective

4

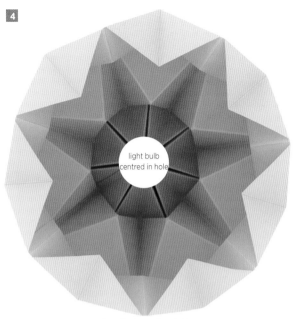

light bulb
centred in hole

lampshade seen from below

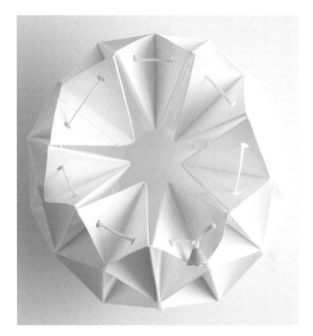

Assembly

Remove the backing from the double-sided tape on the right-hand edge of the folded piece and attach the ends of the model together to create a tube shape, ensuring that the taped edge is on the reverse of the model. To get the best result, press along the double-sided tape strip firmly by compressing the model to the smallest tube shape possible.

Thread a 1 metre length of cord through the punched holes, then gently pull the cord to partially close, and secure the cord ends by tying a sliding knot (see Techniques: Sliding Knot).

Before installing the lampshade, it is important to read the safety instructions (see Techniques: Lamp Safety). Make sure that the power is switched off.

Place the cordset with a light bulb through the opening in the top of the lampshade, then gently pull the cord to tighten. When viewed from below as in Diagram 4, the cord/light bulb should be centred in the hole in the middle of the star shape to ensure that the lampshade hangs straight. Make sure to close the cord at the top completely.

5

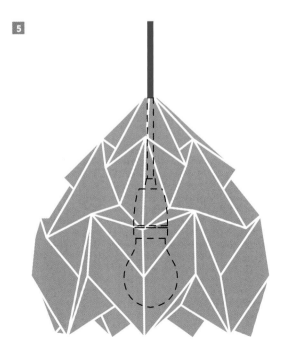

TECHNIQUES

Lamp Safety

When installing or cleaning finished lampshades, it is important to turn off the power first. For the thistle lamp, remove the plug from the wall socket; for any of the ceiling lights, turn off the power at the fuse box.

When fitting a lampshade to a ceiling cordset, make sure you work from a secure set of ladders (or a decorator's platform) and get a friend or family member to hold the ladder so that it stays firmly grounded for extra safety.

The lampshades and light fittings in this book should only be used with LED light bulbs with a maximum wattage of 6 watts. An LED light bulb is energy efficient and heats up less than a halogen or a traditional incandescent light bulb, making it a safe option to use with paper shades.

Some LED lights can produce a cold, bluish light so a paper lampshade can be the perfect choice for these energy-efficient bulbs, as paper makes the light appear more natural, creating a warm, cosy effect, and coloured paper can have a particularly stunning effect on the light.

Although LED light bulbs do not get hot, the light bulb socket can sometimes still get hot depending on the light bulb socket that is used. You should NEVER allow your paper model to come into direct contact with a hot bulb or light bulb socket as this can present a fire risk.

We always recommend that you test your light bulb and light bulb socket first before installing a paper shade. Switch on the light for at least one hour. If after it has been running for one hour you can touch the light bulb and light bulb socket with your hand without burning yourself (be careful!), then it is safe to use with a paper lampshade.

Safety first

- Always use a light bulb and light bulb socket that have been tested and approved to meet the electrical standards of your geographical location. If you cannot be sure of this, buy and replace these products so that they meet these requirements first before installing your paper lampshade.

- Although it is safe to install the paper lampshade yourself, you should ALWAYS have the electric ceiling cord installed by a professional electrician.

- We get the papers that we use for all our products tested for flammability by an official testing lab, and we have found that not all papers are the same. Some types of paper might not meet the safety requirements: when used for lighting, treat the paper you intend to use by soaking or spraying it with a fire retardant treatment.

- Never use a paper lampshade in or near an open fire.

Use a feather duster to clean your paper lampshades.

Folding

There are various methods involved in the folding process, and this section covers the main stages that are covered in the folding instructions for each project.

Basic folds

Before starting to fold, it is important to understand the basics. All of the folded patterns shown in this book are created using just two different types of fold: the mountain fold and the valley fold. These are both simple folds, but they create opposite results.

For the valley fold, you fold the paper in so that the front sides are together, and for the mountain fold, you fold the paper out so that the reverse sides are together.

valley fold   mountain fold

Pre-folding

Before pre-folding, all the lines from the Overview Diagram must first be scored (see How to Use This Book).

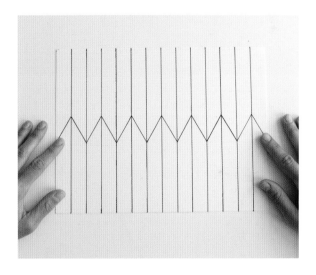

Pre-folding involves folding all of the scored lines as both mountain and valley folds. When a piece of paper is pre-folded it becomes much more flexible and begins to behave more like fabric.

1. Start by pre-folding the vertical lines, and horizontal lines too if marked. Use the edge of a table to fold the lines.

2. Then pre-fold all the diagonals. These are harder to pre-fold as they do not necessarily extend across the whole height or width of the paper. To pre-fold the diagonal lines on either side of a vertical line, valley fold the vertical line so that the diagonal lines overlap.

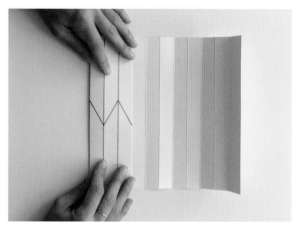

3. Mountain fold along the two overlapping scored diagonal lines.

4. Then valley fold the same lines.

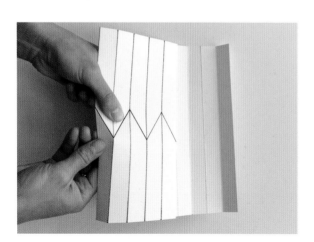

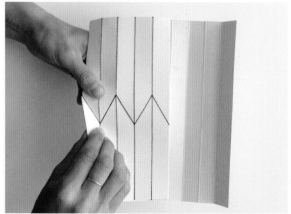

You can use a bone folder to crease the lines, but we prefer to do this by hand.

Pleating

Pleating involves alternating between mountain folds and valley folds to create a concertina shape. This is a basic technique that is used in almost every project in this book. It is important to refer to the Pleating Diagram in the project instructions to identify whether you should start pleating a segment with a valley or mountain fold as this will affect the design. It should be noted that, as you will start pleating at one edge of the paper, this edge of the pleated paper isn't folded and only becomes a valley or mountain fold when the pleated paper is joined with the assembly tab(s). Effectively you cannot fold the first edge of the paper. The Pleating Diagram itself (see How to Use This Book) identifies the orientation of the scored vertical lines in a segment once the paper has been pleated and before the folding steps begin.

To be able to create a pleat, scored, pre-folded vertical lines on the paper are needed as indicated on Diagrams 1 and 2.

While doing the pleating, you will compress the paper to make it easier and quicker to make all the required mountain folds and valley folds. Compressing the paper is just gathering the folded part of the paper in one hand. while pressing the folded part with the other hand (see Photo 1).

After the pleating is completely compressed (Photo 2), you will need to release the paper again to give you the required freedom of movement to be able to change the direction of the folds. In most cases it is enough to just release the paper as in Photo 3, but sometimes you will need to stretch the folded paper a bit as in Photo 4.

1

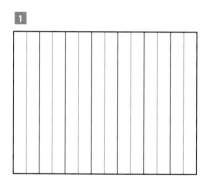

2

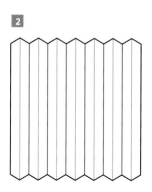

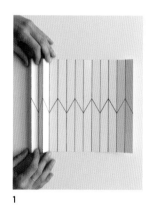

1

2

3

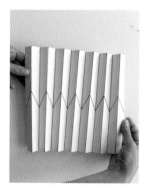

4

Changing direction

Once you have completed the pleating, it is often necessary to change the direction of the vertical folds from a mountain fold to a valley fold or vice versa. The Pleating Diagram shows the orientation of the vertical folds after the paper has been pleated. This is your starting point.

For every folding step, there is a diagram that shows how the direction of the vertical folds for each segment needs to be changed. These diagrams also show that by changing the direction of these vertical folds, the scored diagonal lines in the segment will get the right orientation. The scored diagonal lines will become a mountain or a valley fold by changing the direction of the surrounding vertical folds. The diagram for each folding step shows which scored diagonal lines are affected. These scored diagonal lines will have a blue colour (valley fold) or orange colour (mountain fold).

To make the project text easy to read, the instruction in the project descriptions tells you to mountain fold or valley fold the scored diagonal lines in each segment. What you actually do is change the direction of the vertical folds that surround the scored diagonal lines in this segment. When changing the direction of a vertical fold, from mountain to valley or from valley to mountain, the actual change of the direction of the fold will happen at the intersection between the diagonal lines and the vertical lines.

It is a good idea to practise changing the direction of a vertical fold for a piece of paper with multiple segments before starting to make any of the projects in this book. Changing the direction of the fold is different for every project in this book, depending on the folding pattern. The photos that follow show you how to do this for the pleated paper sample shown, as illustrated in the folding diagram below, Diagram 1, and the step photos will guide you through what to do with your fingers when changing the direction of the fold.

Pleating Diagram

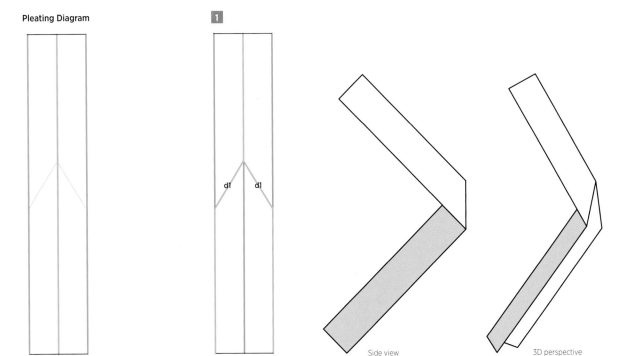

Side view   3D perspective

1. Take your prepared piece of paper, where the lines have been scored, pre-folded and pleated following the Pleating Diagram opposite. Now, to change the direction of the central fold of the first segment from a mountain to a valley fold in the bottom area of the segment (see Diagram 1 opposite), press down with your index finger on the central vertical line below the diagonal scored lines. The central vertical line on the other side of the diagonal scored lines needs to stay as a mountain fold and you can achieve this by holding this part of the paper with your other hand as shown. You will notice that the first diagonal scored line will become a mountain fold.

2. Pinch the part of the central scored vertical line above the diagonal scored lines between your index finger and thumb, whilst simultaneously pushing at point X on the reverse of the paper with the index finger of your other hand.

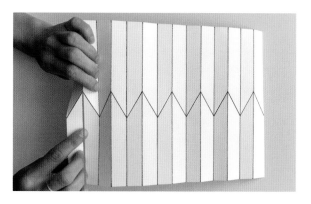

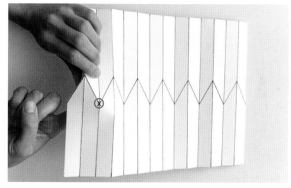

3. Move your finger along the vertical line from point X to the bottom edge of the paper as shown to change this part of the vertical line from a valley to a mountain fold. You will notice that the second diagonal scored line will become a mountain fold.

4. Keep all the folds above the scored diagonal lines in place with one hand as shown, while using the index finger of your other hand to press down on the central vertical line below the diagonal scored lines in the next segment, to make this part into a valley fold.

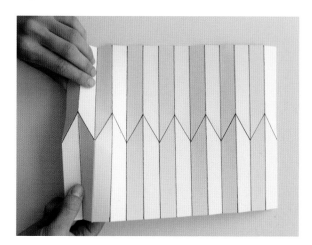

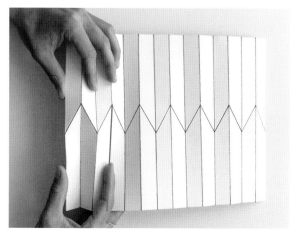

5. Repeat steps 2 and 3 so that the first four scored diagonal lines of the first two segments have become mountain folds. Two segments have now been folded and you can compress the first segment now (do not try to compress both otherwise the paper will wrinkle).

6. Repeat steps 1–5 to work your way along the whole length of the paper, compressing segments as you go.

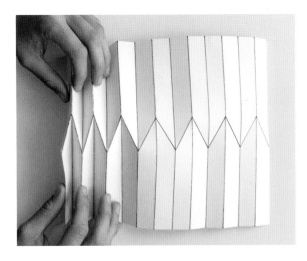

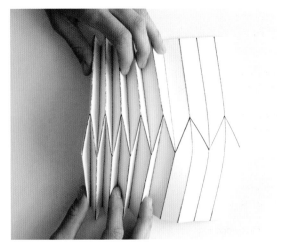

7. When you reach the end of the paper, you can compress the whole model, pressing it firmly to sharpen all the folds. Then release it to create the needed freedom of movement for the next folding step, if the project you are working on has multiple folding steps, or for assembly.

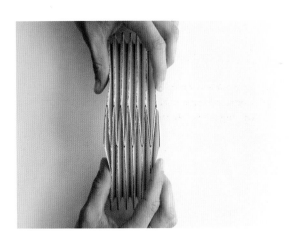

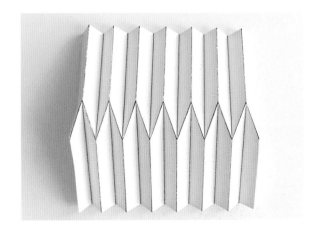

Sliding Knot

The sliding knot is used to secure the ends of a length of cord and it allows a folded model to be opened to insert a new battery or to replace a light bulb.

1. Use a hole punch to punch holes along the edge of the folded piece of paper following the instructions for the project.

2. Thread a 1 metre length of cord through the holes and make an overhand knot at one end of the cord (labelled a on Diagram 1). Pull tight to secure (see Diagram 2).

3. Make another overhand knot next to the first knot (see Diagram 3). Before pulling the second knot tight, thread the other end of the cord (labelled b on Diagram 3) through the second knot (see Diagram 4).

4. Slide the second knot along the cord so that it is positioned next to the first knot and pull the end of the cord (labelled b on Diagram 5) through the second knot to tighten. This enables you to open and close the paper model.

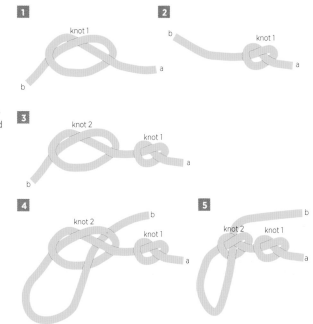

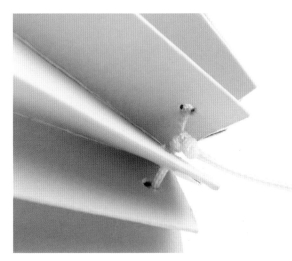

Where it is not necessary to open a folded model, a third knot can be tied close to knot 2 and the cord ends can be trimmed.

Templates

All templates are shown at full size.
You can download printable versions of these templates from: http://ideas.sewandso.co.uk/patterns.

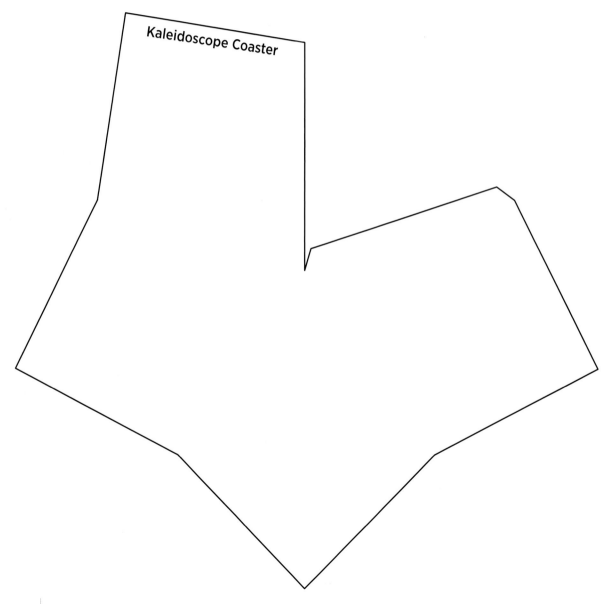

Kaleidoscope Coaster

Window
Decoration

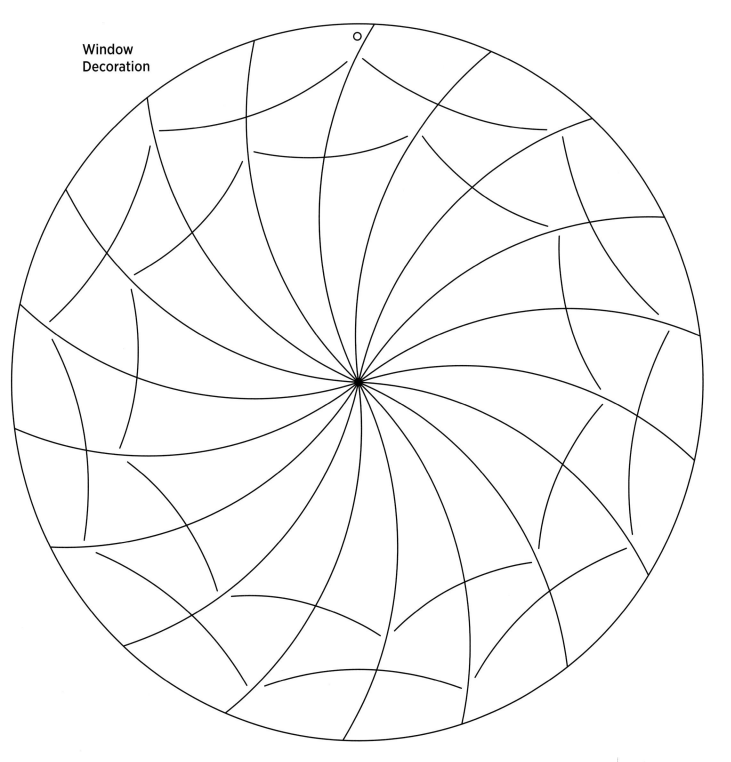

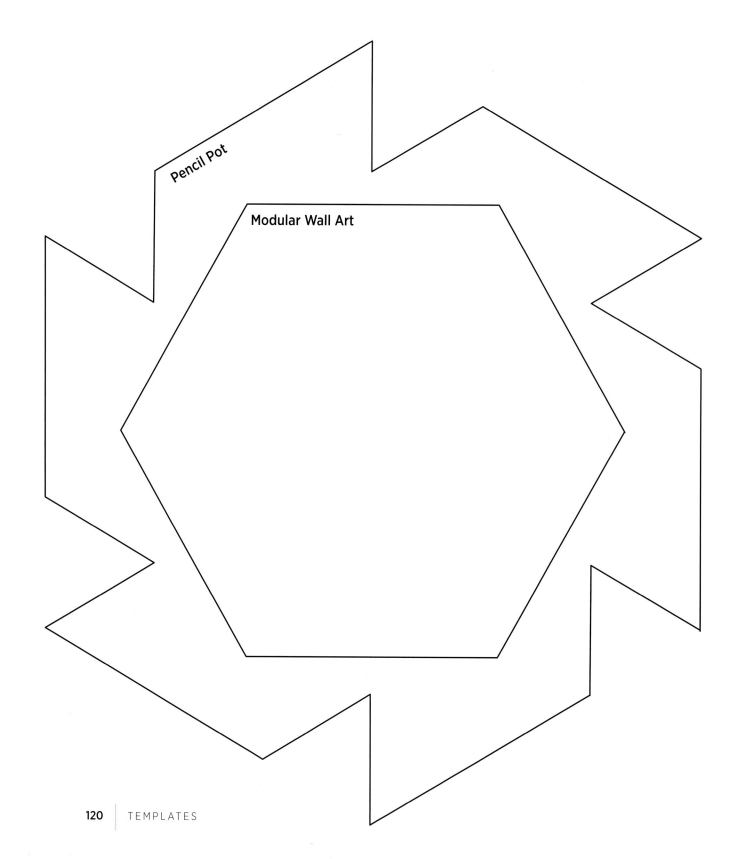

Pencil Pot

Modular Wall Art

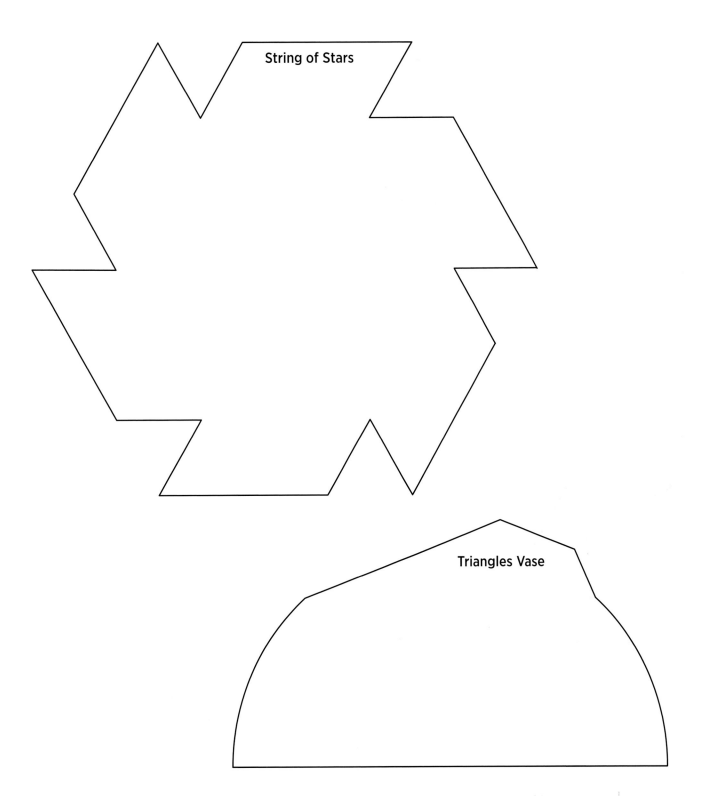

String of Stars

Triangles Vase

Leaf Mobile

Wave Lampshade
Part A

Join to Part B

Wave
Lampshade
Part B

Join to Part A

Join to Part C

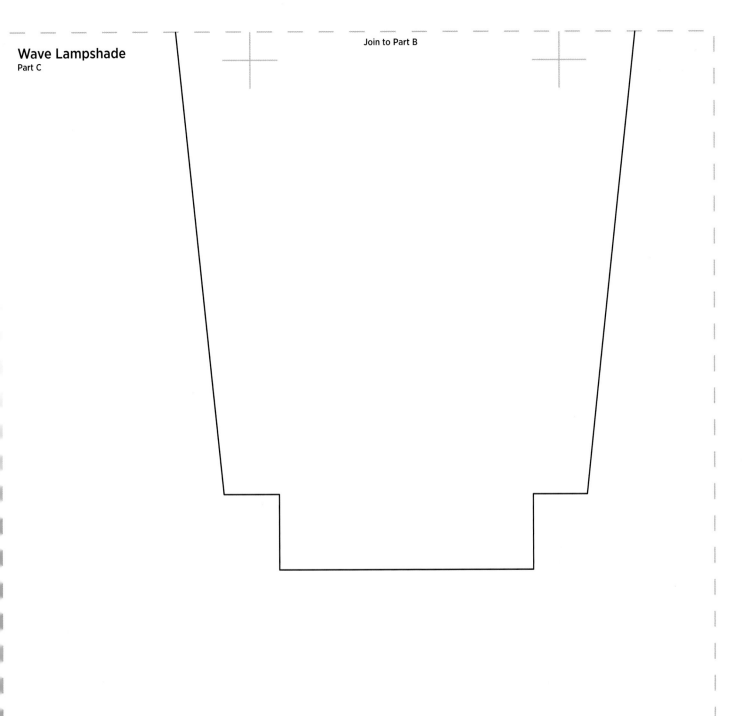

Wave Lampshade
Part C

Join to Part B

About the Authors

Nellianna van den Baard and Kenneth Veenenbos are the designers behind Studio Snowpuppe. Since 2010 they have been designing and producing origami lampshades mainly from paper. Their work has been sold and published worldwide.

Nellianna studied architecture in Delft and went to Sweden for six months to study abroad. After her studies she went to work as an architect for a couple of years.

Kenneth studied industrial design in Delft and has been a passionate windsurfer since he was a teenager. After his studies he went to work as a designer for a shipyard for one year. After that he did some freelance work, but soon started to work on his own products. His first designs were an aerodynamic umbrella and a clever toothbrush holder. From this experience he learned that he wanted to design more sustainable products that are made by hand.

Nellianna and Kenneth met each other as students. After their studies they lived in Scheveningen, a coastal village. In 2015 they moved to the historic city centre of Brielle, a very old, fortified town.

When they are not working, Nellianna and Kenneth enjoy going to the beach, or the dunes, together with their kids.

BETTER LIVING THROUGH ORIGAMI

Thanks

We want to thank SewandSo for contacting us: writing this book was a new challenge and we are happy that we have had this opportunity.

We want to thank our kids for distracting us with their play.

This book would never have been written if we had not started our studio, so we would like to thank all the people who helped with this:

We would like to dedicate this book to Nellianna's father. On his birthday in 2010 we gave him an origami project – this turned out to be the starting point for our folding adventure.

Thanks to Nellianna's mother, who taught her to live sober and to help others. This has given us the opportunity to be creative.
Thanks to Kenneth's father for listening to all of his creative ideas.
Thanks to Kenneth's mother for raising him with wooden toys.
Thanks to Edwin Pelser for helping us to launch our first lamp.
Thanks to Frank Vlasveld for advice on paper.
Thanks to Coen de Ridder and Ramses Duin from Plasticarto for advice on die-cutting.
Thanks to Jochem Goldschmidt for coming up with the name Snowpuppe.
Thanks to our customers and loyal fans.

Suppliers

There is an online space dedicated to this book. It includes links to suppliers as well as additional tips, full size templates and resources. Please find it here: www.studiosnowpuppe.nl/betterlivingthroughorigami

Index

ISBN-13: 978-1-4463-0712-0 paperback
SRN: R7787 paperback

ISBN-13: 978-1-4463-7669-0 PDF
SRN: R7959 PDF

ISBN-13: 978-1-4463-7668-3 EPUB
SRN: R7958 EPUB

Printed in China by RR Donnelley for:
F&W Media International, Ltd
Pynes Hill Court, Pynes Hill, Exeter, EX2 5AZ, UK

10 9 8 7 6 5 4 3 2 1

Content Director: Ame Verso
Managing Editor: Jeni Hennah
Project Editor: Cheryl Brown
Design Manager: Lorraine Inglis
Art Direction: Prudence Rogers and Ilona Zieltjens
Photographers: Jason Jenkins and Stan Koolen
Production Manager: Beverley Richardson

F&W Media publishes high quality books on a wide range of subjects.
For more great book ideas visit: www.sewandso.co.uk

Layout of the digital edition of this book may vary depending on reader hardware and display settings.